JETHRO TULL

..Into The Eighties

Laura Shenton

JETHRO TULL

..Into The Eighties

Laura Shenton

WP
WYMER
PUBLISHING
Bedford, England

First published in 2023 by Wymer Publishing
Bedford, England www.wymerpublishing.co.uk Tel: 01234 326691
Wymer Publishing is a trading name of Wymer (UK) Ltd

Print edition (fully illustrated): **ISBN: 978-1-915246-40-0**

Edited by Jerry Bloom.

eBook formatting by Coinlea.
Printed and bound in Great Britain by
CMP, Dorset.

A catalogue record for this book is available from the British Library.

Typeset by Andy Bishop / Tusseheia Creative
Cover design by Tusseheia Creative

Contents

"Making a new Jethro Tull album is applying yourself to not disappointing the fans, and at the same time, giving them something new."
Ian Anderson, 1982

8

"I suppose we've lost some of the people who first heard us, but the damage couldn't be too severe. The audiences on our current tour have been fantastic."
Martin Barre, 1987

Preface

By the 1980s, the landscape of popular music had changed significantly. The late seventies had introduced a plethora of genres to the record-buying public. With disco, punk and new wave (to name a few!) having been championed by the mainstream music press and critics, bands who had thrived from the late sixties onwards could no longer take it for granted that they would have the same appeal and level of success.

With albums such as *Aqualung* (1971), *Thick As A Brick* (1972) and *Songs From The Wood* (1977) to Jethro Tull's credit, it is understandable as to why so many fans regard the seventies as the band's peak. However, it would certainly be a missed opportunity for any fan to write off Tull's 1980s output as being unworthy in comparison; although in the grand scheme of things it may not receive the same level of recognition as their critically acclaimed and commercially successful output of the 1970s, it still holds merit that is worthy of research and engagement.

Whilst the 1970s line-ups of Jethro Tull made their mark on the musical map as one of the most innovative, influential and unique progressive rock bands of the era, there is value in recognising the validity and relevance of the band's work in the 1980s, which was marked by a change in sound and style.

Straight after 1979's *Stormwatch*, with yet another

line-up change, Jethro Tull underwent a significant evolution in their musical approach. The Ian Anderson-led band shifted away from the complex and intricate progressive rock arrangements of the 1970s and embraced a more streamlined and accessible sound that incorporated elements of folk, blues, and hard rock. While this change in direction may have been initially polarising amongst fans and critics, it resulted in some of the band's most memorable and commercially successful albums, including *The Broadsword And The Beast* (1982) and *Crest Of A Knave* (1987) (which earned the band their famously controversial and highly debated Grammy).

Furthermore, the 1980s saw Jethro Tull experimenting with new instrumentation and incorporating more electronic elements into their music. Amongst this, their exploration of themes and lyrical content remained just as engaging as when they had explored topics such as environmentalism, social issues, and personal introspection in their 1970s music. Overall, 1980s Jethro Tull maintained the same artistic scope that had helped to solidify their reputation as a versatile and forward-thinking band.

Every Tull fan has their favourite album(s) and a lot of that probably goes towards some of the excitement of talking with each other about it. There are always new and interesting points of view to consider. All the same, in writing this book, it matters to me to maintain a narrative that is objective rather than something that's based on my own opinions. As a result, you'll be seeing a range of quotes from vintage and contemporary resources, the aim being to provide an authentic portrayal of how the band's music and performances were received at the time.

As the long-term leader of Jethro Tull, Ian Anderson has always done most of the public speaking on behalf of the band. The proportion of band member quotes in this book is therefore reflective of that. And in the interest of continued transparency, as I have mentioned in my previous books on Jethro Tull, I have no affiliation with anyone from the band and/or any of their associates.

By examining and celebrating Jethro Tull's music of the 1980s, the purpose of this book is to provide scope for further appreciation of the band's evolution and the ways in which they continued to push boundaries and innovate. Also, considering that at the time of writing, the band is still going, there is value in putting Jethro Tull's 1980s material under the spotlight in acknowledgement of its significant artistic and cultural merit.

14

A

The eighties got off to an uncertain start for Jethro Tull. A month-long European tour began in mid-March promoting 1979's *Stormwatch*. It concluded on 14th April following a five-night stint at London's Hammersmith Odeon. Ian Anderson was already thinking ahead. "All of us in the group had individual projects that we wanted to follow — not necessarily all musical, but domestic as well," he said. "I've never played with any other musicians. I've only played with the people in Jethro Tull."

Consequently, drummer Barrie "Barriemore" Barlow, keyboardists John Evan and David (now Dee) Palmer were out of the band, and with the unfortunate passing of bassist John Glascock the previous year due to heart complications, the first album of the eighties — *A* — featured a brand new line-up alongside frontman Ian Anderson and guitarist Martin Barre.

The album marked Tull's first recorded appearance of Fairport Convention's Dave Pegg (who had filled in for Glascock during the band's 1979 tour). Mark Craney played drums and credited as a "special guest", Eddie Jobson played keyboards and electric violin.

There are conflicting accounts as to why John Evan, David Palmer and Barrie Barlow left Jethro Tull. However, the version of events stating that Anderson had already stipulated that he wanted to take Jethro Tull in a new musical direction and away from the folk and progressive rock of the 1970s, is certainly a plausible one — especially when comparing *Stormwatch* to *A*. "With the old line-up, nobody was under the impression that we were going to necessarily just continue on and on and on doing the Jethro Tull thing," he said.

Notably, the line-up of Jethro Tull that features on *A* was perhaps more a result of convenience than of a recruitment of musicians intended to be long-term members of the band.

Eddie Jobson had always maintained that he was only going to be a guest musician for Jethro Tull, and even then, as one thing led to another, he made it clear even to the music press that his time with the band would be up following the end of the tour to promote *A*. "I owe it to myself to try to achieve something on my own without the protection of a big name," he said. Notably, his previous band U.K. — with varying line-ups featuring John Wetton, Bill Bruford, Allan Holdsworth and Terry Bozzio — had been another casualty of the turn of the decade, unable to appeal to an audience that was looking for a post-prog rock sound. Jobson candidly admitted this to *Melody Maker* in 1980, stating that U.K. was "doing well in America and Japan, and for a while I thought it was going to be big" but that ultimately, they were "too old-fashioned. Everybody was re-evaluating what they were going to do over the next ten years and I didn't see that U.K. had a future. The music was very seventies."

Jobson had planned for his time with Tull to be temporary simply due to the fact that he was at something of a crossroads in his career. As he explained to *Melody*

Maker; "I was saying to Ian the other night that I've been doing the professional big circuit in big bands like Zappa or Roxy — but always on somebody else's back. Now I'm off again with Jethro Tull, and it's time I sat down and planned my career properly. The period with Ian Anderson is not permanent. I know what will happen when I leave by next April — people will think I'm being stupid and say I can't hold a job down. It's simply that I don't want a permanent association with something that is considered fairly old-fashioned, even though it is updating itself. I think that's a negative thing, and the very reason I disbanded U.K.."

Although Ian Anderson has always been at the forefront of Jethro Tull, when Jobson came to work with him for *A*, he brought his own opinions and ideas about how the band should progress. "I've joined bands and had to play a little on the leader's terms," he said. "But this time, half the reason I was invited was because Ian wanted me to come in as myself and offer a new dimension. A free hand! No holds barred! None of the Ye Olde Englande, olde worlde Jethro Tull thing. I couldn't have gone along with that. I just don't like looking back too much. I don't think a rock musician can afford to."

Mark Craney joined Jethro Tull as a direct result of having played on the audition tape that Eddie Jobson had submitted to the band. Upon hearing the tape and being impressed with the drumming, Anderson asked Jobson to bring Craney on board. Prior to that, Craney had played on jazz rock violinist Jean-Luc Ponty's album, *Imaginary Voyage* (1976), and also as a member of the Tommy Bolin band. Like Bolin, Craney had also grown up in Iowa's Sioux City/Sioux Falls area.

Having been fully aware of the strain that the band dynamics were under prior to the big split, and cautious about where to place his allegiances, Martin Barre eventually concluded that on the basis that audiences had come to expect Jethro Tull to be Ian Anderson and friends, there was no harm in sticking with it (and even then, the decision could have gone either way!). "The new line-up has given Jethro Tull the kiss of life," he told *Melody Maker*. "Things work so well between us that I feel completely refreshed. I could never join another group, but I could have stopped playing last year quite easily. I also felt that even if Ian was re-forming, he should get a fresh guitar player for his own sake. We'd been together too long."

Recorded at Maison Rouge (the mobile studio at Anderson's Buckinghamshire home — where the band rode motorbikes and shot clay pigeons in between work — and in the main studio building in London), *A* was originally made with the intention of it being Anderson's debut solo release. This is reflected in the album's title, as the master tapes were labelled with the letter "A" for Anderson. "I just wanted to take a break from the band and do something different, and I wanted to see if working with other people might make the music take on a different sound or feel," he said.

All the same, Chrysalis Records insisted that the album should be released under the Jethro Tull name. Anderson said, "Terry Ellis persuaded me that this should be a Jethro Tull album because I had Martin on it, and because Terry thought a solo album should just be me plunking on a guitar by myself. So I let myself be persuaded."

Anderson told *Trouser Press* in 1982: "*A* became a Jethro Tull record at the behest of the record company and against my better judgement; it was originally to be a solo album of mine. It continued what *Stormwatch* started, much more electronic and concerned with current affairs. It was written around news broadcasts, things I'd read about in the paper that morning, written about that day and rehearsed with what accidentally became a band that afternoon. It was put together very quickly in a terrific atmosphere of people playing together and being challenged by each other's abilities. I really enjoyed making it. I didn't enjoy finishing it, mixing it, because I felt very nervous about calling it a Jethro Tull album. The actual recording of it was great."

With an increased use of synthesisers and a greater emphasis on electronic rock, *A* marked a significant musical shift from Jethro Tull's previous albums. Anderson said in later years that the album "was mainly to be a foray into a more hard-edged electric and less quaint music that energised me to write and arrange the material".

However, the characteristic folk influences and Anderson's flute were still present. Lyrically, the album was a departure from the fantasy and folklore themes of earlier Tull works, instead focusing on more contemporary issues, particularly the Cold War.

For some fans, the change of musical style was a point of controversy, with many having come to expect a certain trademark sound. Vitally though, the album is still distinctively the work of Ian Anderson's Jethro Tull, as is particularly apparent on the track 'The Pine Marten's Jig'.

The majority of the tracks on *A* were composed specifically for it. A few were written in the three-week gap between the end of the *Stormwatch* tour and starting work on the new album. Other songs were created in the rehearsal room whilst the album was being recorded. Despite the fact that he already had some pre-existing material written, Anderson's aim was to be flexible. By not referring to ideas that he had already come up with previously, he reasoned that it would allow for creative freedom and a more collaborative approach between the musicians in the studio. Not only that, but it left their options open in terms of being able to explore a more diverse range of musical styles.

"There's no set theme to the album," said Anderson. "But I do feel the metre is good and so are the rhymes. The words aren't the usual hackneyed variety you find in rock songs. They're simply a decent set of lyrics that nobody has written yet. And those are what I always try to write."

For the most part, a lot of the material on previous Jethro Tull albums had been written whilst on tour. Anderson estimated that with *A*, there were only about four songs where this was the case. He found it invigorating that with the line-up he had acquired for the album, he could write a song in the morning, rehearse it in the afternoon, and record it at night. The result was spontaneity rather than arrangements that had already been decided upon.

For the song that became 'Crossfire', Anderson already had the title and a vague idea of the lyrics in mind. During the band's rehearsal of it, they were interrupted when his wife urgently informed them that the Iranian

Embassy in London was under siege. They immediately stopped to watch the news coverage on television. The following morning, before the rest of the band had arrived for rehearsal, Anderson completed the song's lyrics. Although 'Crossfire' had previously been heading in a similar thematic direction, it was the news event that inspired him to write the remainder of the lyrics.

The inspiration for 'Fylingdale Flyer' also came from a news story: one where the Americans had a minor issue with one of their early warning systems and consequently suspected a Russian attack. The lyrics are from the perspective of the personnel at the Fylingdale Early Warning Station in Yorkshire. They observe a missile heading towards America, but it is only halfway there, giving them time to determine the severity of the situation. In a nod to Sir Francis Drake's reaction upon hearing news of the Spanish Armada's approach in 1588, they decide to have a "last quick game of bowls." The song was released as a single, as was the album's following track.

Anderson wrote 'Working John, Working Joe' a couple of years prior to recording *A*. The song was written during a period when unions were heavily criticising the middle class. The slightly humorous track implies that the white-collar worker, who serves as a company director, has an equally demanding daily routine as the blue-collar worker on the factory floor. Despite driving to work, he still encounters traffic congestion, and the dilemma that his pursuit of wealth comes with consequences to his health. ("Not that there's anything wrong with working-class lyrics," Anderson told *Melody Maker*. "But I maintain that there are classes in our society, and I do write from a certain standpoint, and it would be silly to pretend I didn't.")

Anderson penned the lyrics for 'Black Sunday' just before going on a previous tour. They are reflective of his mood at the time but refer to a universally relatable feeling that would resonate with anyone who goes to work and is constantly anxious to return home to find everything unchanged. Throughout the song, there is reference to the things that Anderson witnessed while travelling.

The title 'Protect And Survive' is derived from a government-issued pamphlet of the same name, which provided a brief outline of what to do in the event of a nuclear attack. The song contains a slightly humorous jab at the government for not having provided sufficient information and for treating the public poorly. When promoting *A*, Anderson noted that although the song's sentiments were not necessarily a reflection of his own, he believed that they served to capture what the average person's reaction would be upon reading such a pamphlet, particularly in the aftermath of a nuclear attack.

'Batteries Not Included' is a rather dark song. It tells the story of a child who wakes up on Christmas morning to find a magnificent mechanical toy at the foot of their bed. Unfortunately, the toy fails to operate due to the absence of batteries. While the child contemplates the toy's lack of functionality, they become so deeply connected to it that when their parents wake up, they find that the child has become like the toy, immobile and switched off. The song features Anderson's son Jamie, who made his recording debut on the track.

Although 'The Pine Marten's Jig' sounds like a traditional piece of music, it incorporates several intricate time signature changes. The instrumentation, consisting of mandolins and violins, is fairly traditional, but the combination yields an electrifying outcome.

'Uniform' presents a light-hearted approach to the idea that everyone assumes a role in society based on their attire, and that most people tend to conform to certain social groups and rarely express their individuality through dress, ultimately wearing uniforms just like those in authoritative occupations.

'4.W.D. (Low Ratio)' is essentially an ode to the love of four-wheel-drive vehicles, with Anderson simply saying at the time that it was "nice to have a song about that."

'And Further On' is ambiguous and wistful. When promoting *A*, Anderson maintained that the song held private and personal significance but hoped that it was broad enough to have appeal to others. "To specifically explain my understanding of the lyric would be to rob the individual of his right to a personal interpretation," he said. "I suppose it really serves as a musical and lyrical postscript to the rest of the songs on the album."

The Cincinnati Post asserted that "*A* sounds like a great beginning for a revitalised Jethro Tull", whilst saying of the new line-up; "This reshuffling has achieved a minor miracle — a slight change in the Jethro Tull sound, which has been exactly the same stodgy brand of art-rock or thought-rock for twelve years. The change isn't that overpowering or radical, but it shows some enlightenment on Anderson's part."

From Texas newspaper, *The Marshall News Messenger*: "What happens to rock 'n' rollers when they get too old to rock 'n' roll? Actually, there is no set answer.

Performers like Chuck Berry keep playing, though they don't write anymore. Others, like Janis Joplin, Elvis Presley and Keith Moon, live too hard, too fast and pass away. Bands such as The Stones, Led Zeppelin, and The Who somehow keep their creative juices flowing and add to their rock legends. Unfortunately, Jethro Tull falls into a category of old rock bands which continue to cut albums but have no creativity. Ian Anderson, who for all practical purposes is Jethro Tull, is simply not the songwriter who recorded *Thick As A Brick*, *Minstrel In The Gallery*, *Aqualung*, and the still-remarkable 'Bourée'."

"In 1977, Anderson made the change from a driving rock sound to a more sophisticated keyboard sound. While the change might have suited Anderson's age, it didn't suit many of his fans. The new songs were poorly received in concert until stage performances continued to emphasise the older music. Since *Songs From The Wood* in 1977, Tull has released three studio albums, each worse than the last. Tull's latest release, *A*, continues the downward trend with only fleeting glimpses of the band's glorious past. The songs are covered with synthesiser sludge, and most of the tunes are basically unlistenable."

"The album desperately needs a sense of direction. Two of the tunes are the worst I've heard Anderson write. One called '4.W.D. (Low Ratio)' sounds like Ted Nugent should have recorded it. And 'Batteries Not Included' is a childish song about a kid with a new toy and no batteries. Two songs barely rise above mediocrity. 'Fylingdale Flyer' is the closest the band comes to a rocker and the guitar work by Martin Barre almost overcomes the idiotic lyrics. The best song on the LP is 'And Further On'. The slow passages of the cut are reminiscent of the sounds

Anderson used so effectively on *Minstrel In The Gallery*. Anderson sounds like the Ian of old, a welcome relief from the rest of the album."

"*A* dramatically illustrates Anderson's loss of passion for performing — both musically and lyrically. His songs have become a dull monotone, lacking enthusiasm or emotion. So Anderson, one of the most eccentric in his culture, continues to stubbornly hold on to his new sound despite dwindling sales. Unless something changes, Anderson may never again record a song to get excited about. Many of the old Jethro Tull albums have worn thin with play. I'm sure though, *A* will join many of Tull's latest releases, which haven't spent much time out of their jackets. Nothing's perfect, but Anderson is definitely "too old to rock 'n' roll: too young to die"."

From *Record Mirror*: "Jethro Tull have come up with a good concept for their new album. Many of the tracks are lyrically dealing with events that take place in the news every day. And what's more, it's effective. For instance, the first song on side one, 'Crossfire', is the most up-to-date concerning the siege of the Iranian Embassy in London... Apart from the good idea and lyrics, the track itself features a terrific guitar and flute instrumental sequence, and excellent vocals, both lead and backing (I could hear every word)… A lot of tracks show the band's recognition of the threat of nuclear attack… The vocal harmonies that are perhaps one of the trademarks of Tull are perfect… Most of the songs on the album have a very high quality and they grow on you with repeated playing."

From *Melody Maker*: "Twelve years on the road with a sound that has not radically changed was a long time for Ian Anderson, so when it was announced a few weeks ago that Jethro Tull was to be reborn, with interesting new musicians added while some old faithfuls would leave, the prospect was good. This, then, is the new Jethro Tull, with keyboardists John Evan and David Palmer gone, along with drummer Barrie Barlow. The new men are Mark Craney (drums) and "special guest" Eddie Jobson at the keyboards and on electric violin. It's good to see Martin Barre, the outstanding guitarist, remains, as does the fine bassist Dave Pegg."

"The transformation is remarkable. Whether the infusion of new talent alone has motivated Anderson to write more potently and sing with greater conviction, or whether a mere fresh touch by different players has worked on his psyche for the better, is difficult to perceive. Whatever, the result is an album that continues Anderson's preoccupation with environmental excesses (after the last LP, *Stormwatch*, and its focus on North Sea oil), but in an altogether more lyrical and communicative style. The old band, on reflection, seems heavy-handed, if able; the new line-up, particularly through the virtuosity of Eddie Jobson, has a deftness, a lightness of touch, that has been missing for years."

"All the songs are by Anderson, with "additional musical material" by Jobson; and the arrangements are credited to the whole band. The urgency and extra touches may have been co-operative, but there's little doubt that Anderson's is the dominant theme. The sleeve picture depicts the band in the control tower, presumably as a commentary on the song 'Fylingdale Flyer', a wry tilt at the danger in our midst. This, however, seems a pretty lightweight song to carry the title of the record. Better songs by far are 'Working John, Working Joe', in which Anderson is at his observant best, touching on the role of the businessman who 'commutes eighty miles a day…'."

"And 'Uniform' is one of his finest, most incisive lyrics, pointing out the obvious — that everyone from traffic wardens to city workers to Muslims in "white bed sheets" is in a uniform of some kind. The violin work of Jobson here is at its peak, lending a great urgency to a song which, like all the best, is very simple. 'And Further On', which ends with the question: "will we still be here further on?", and 'Protect And Survive', are in the same vein of questioning progress, while 'Batteries Not Included' is a masterly stab at the unimportance of Japanese toys, with this lunging finale: 'Mummy, Daddy, can't hear you, batteries not included in this little boy'."

"What makes Anderson and Jethro Tull difficult for some to comprehend is that he's working well outside the accepted macho rock formula yet within a rock music framework: the concept of this album, following *Heavy Horses* and *Songs From The Wood*, confirm an allegiance to folk music as much as to rock; it's good to hear a composer writing something serious, as opposed to 'I Love My Baby.' And he leaves a lot to be read between the lines by the listener, making the discovery on repeated playing more rewarding. The precision in songwriting and the diligence of this record, marking a newly injected burst of energy in one of Britain's best bands, make it convincing and refreshing."

From *Musicians Only*: "Well, after all the confusion and personnel changes, it still sounds like Tull, albeit with some subtle differences. The substitution of two keyboards (John Evan and David Palmer) by one

Eddie Jobson has currently enough resulted in a greater emphasis on keyboards because the new man is a more pushy and upfront musician than his predecessors. Mark Craney is more straightforward and less driving than Barrie Barlow, but does his job well enough. Dave Pegg is a looser, more adaptable bassist than the late John Glascock, who only managed to complete three tracks on the last album, *Stormwatch*."

"'Crossfire' is a sombre, forceful tune given dark menace by Pegg's sub-disco walking bass and Jobson's active piano. Several listens to 'Fylingdale Flyer' have failed to unearth any genuine melody, though it is notable for its sinuous flute/synth bridge backed by pounding bass and sharp on/off drumbeats. Although 'Working John, Working Joe' opens with acoustic guitar, it turns out to be a bludgeoning piece that hammers home its point mercilessly. 'Black Sunday' is a dull song that consequently turns into a feature for Jobson's lightning piano and atmospheric synth. 'Protect And Survive' is a poke at the ridiculous government pamphlet of the same name that tells you what to do when they drop the bomb, and works well against its hesitant backdrop. Another success is 'Batteries Not Included', driving, snarling and deliberately inhuman. Jobson's electric violin follows Anderson's vocal line on 'Uniform' before emerging in its own right. Despite its modern instrumentation, '4.W.D. (Low Ratio)' is about as close to a blues as the band has come since *This Was*. 'The Pine Marten's Jig' is full of cripplingly awkward time changes, and leads the way to a typically mellow Anderson closer, 'And Further On'. After the fine "rustic" albums *Songs From The Wood* and *Heavy Horses*, Tull lost their way with the disappointing *Stormwatch*. This set does not redress the balance but does demonstrate that this is a line-up with some potential."

As Jethro Tull's thirteenth studio album, *A* was released in August 1980 in the UK, and in the September of the same year in the US. It got to number twenty-five in the UK, to number thirty in the US, and was welcomed by many critics. However, due to the way in which the band had changed, it certainly managed to divide opinion amongst long-time fans. With a new musical direction and also, a new line-up, it signified what could be considered a new era for Jethro Tull.

***

The tour to promote *A* covered Europe and America, with the band only doing two London dates in the UK. (Fortunately, there was the release of *Slipstream*. The first official Jethro Tull home video, it includes footage of the tour as well as studio promos. Released in 2021, the fortieth anniversary boxset of *A* features not only the album remixed by Steven Wilson, but several bonus tracks, and an audio recording of a concert that took place in Los Angeles — all as well as a DVD of *Slipstream*.)

Before setting off on tour, Anderson had put thought into the setlist in a way that was mindful of audience expectations. "On tour we'll obviously be playing the songs that are well known Jethro Tull classics that people expect us to play," he said. "If I went to see The Kinks, Led Zeppelin, The Who, or Frank Sinatra, I'd be upset if they didn't play those one or two songs that to me are "the ones", and that are still magic no matter how many times I hear them. So I assume people feel the same way about Jethro Tull."

So, who was Jethro Tull's audience by this point in the band's tenure? According to Anderson: "We really have been thankfully able to pull them in. We lose them at the top end because there is that old story that they have a wife and two kids and a mortgage to support. But we're getting younger audiences all the time, and although sales of catalogue albums are generally down in the record business at the moment, ours are doing consistently well. *Aqualung* has done about four-million and is still going, and they must be being bought by youngish people. So I don't accept that the band's audience is ageing."

With *A* being a relatively new sound for Jethro Tull, and with some of the musicians being new to the band, it was inevitable that those factors needed to be taken into account when preparing for the tour. "To two of the band, it's a completely new show," said Anderson. "In the past, we have had the core of the material from the past and rehearsing it was just sort of stimulating the memory buds again, but this time, we're going to have to put a lot more work into rehearsing the show. Two-thirds of the show will be relatively new material. There might be half-an-hour to forty minutes' worth of material that people are familiar with from previous Jethro Tull line-ups, but there will be all of the new album, and there will be some more new material specially written for the tour, plus members of the band doing solo spots, which are their contribution pieces which they will have written or put together."

"I am sure that in terms of our presentation on stage, we'll probably move a little bit away from the kind of thing Jethro Tull has been doing in the past, and which tends to be a bit historical. It's always felt — and I am sure it looked like — we were low-key Village People on stage being dressed up in very definitive styles of clothing that had nothing to do with each other. With this album being a tight and quickly-put-together affair, there is a validity in presenting this in a more uniform sort of basis, since the group does play well as a group and will make more of a contribution as a group on stage. Once we get up there, my part of the thing is just one of the group. I may be more to the fore than the others, but it's still a group entity, and it's all a great irony considering the fact that the album was supposed to be a solo album in the first place. It's turned out to be more of a group album than many of the previous Jethro Tull albums."

Musing upon the question of whether or not Jethro Tull was relevant to the new decade, *Melody Maker* considered in October 1980; "It depends entirely on how we measure relevance. To about thirteen-thousand people who will see their two London concerts, and half a million people who will attend their worldwide shows, and enjoy them enough to go and buy Tull's old and new albums, the band is relevant. Judged against, say, The Teardrop Explodes or The Pretenders, Jethro Tull take on a positively paternal, nay grandfatherly, look. Ian Anderson is under no illusions. He's thirty-three, married with two children, a landowner and active conservationist and fish farmer whose whole standpoint seems far removed from the world of rock. But yes, the reason he's relevant, and people continue to support Jethro Tull, is that they exist outside the generally accepted rock ethic. They are into music, and that doesn't necessarily mean they have to

SUNDAY EXTRA

The world knows him as Ian Anderson, demonic singer of the top rock band Jethro Tull. But he has another life, as JIM CRACE reports.

Skye has no limits for its new Laird

"Och, he's doing a grand job up there at Kilmarie," says one of the younger and more generous of the islanders of Skye as the new Laird of Strathaird is glimpsed bumping along the single track road to his 15,000-acre estate.

"It's good to see an outsider coming in and putting money and life back into the land."

The Laird himself, puffing so untiringly on a curly pipe that his deerstalker and old brown shooting jacket are sweet with the odour of tobacco, would like to spend much more time at Kilmarie House; would even like to become a regular unremarked face on the island of Skye.

But for the moment duties elsewhere are keeping him away from the Strathaird Estate.

Islanders who have not met the master of Kilmarie in person will probably have been among the world-wide audience of about 400 million who watched him on television recently.

Relayed live by satellite from Madison Square Garden in New York, the Laird leapt about the stage in knee-length tartan cloak, tam o'shanter, white trousers, leather boots and cod-piece.

Wild-haired and pop-eyed, evidently kept earthbound only by his tight grip on the microphone stand, he conjured a breathless sequence from his flute which hushed the audience to reverential silence.

For the new Laird of Strathaird is Ian Anderson, 32 years old, leader, singer, songwriter and flautist with the rock band Jethro Tull, which has sold 20 million record albums in the past 12 years. The latest LP **Stormwatch** has already sold more than a million copies in the US where the group has enjoyed its most enduring popularity.

Indeed, Jethro Tull's recent tour of America was its most successful and "highest grossing" yet. Every concert (in 20-30,000-seat auditoria) was a sell-out.

Anderson's stage act has earned him the title of "the deranged flamingo of rock". "It's part of the celebration of people gathering together to hear music," he says.

"We draw on anything from rock and roll to quiet acoustic pieces. My original impetus was black American music, but I'm not black and I'm not American, so I won't slavishly follow its styles.

"I sing in my own voice with a British accent. And when I'm in skyscraper hotels on tour in the US I'm writing English 'country songs."

Now he has a large piece of British countryside to himself, but he denies that the Skye estate is just the passing fancy of a man with too much cash to spare. It is, he says, the fulfilment of a lifelong ambition.

"I wouldn't say I have always been interested in agriculture, but I did have an interest in the countryside, in the childhood spirit of being outdoors.

"Agriculture is now the rationale by which I can justify indulging myself in the outdoors. But as an adult it would be a selfish sort of luxury to buy land for use simply as a playground. I have to find some way of using land that will conserve the best of it."

Ian Anderson was born in 1947 in Dunfermline, where his father ran a small hotel. But the family (he has two brothers — one is now the administrator of the Scottish Ballet for whom Ian has recently composed some music) soon moved to Edinburgh and then to Blackpool.

Popular rock mythology has it that he paid early tribute to his farming interests by naming his group after Jethro Tull, the 18th-century agricultural innovator who wrote The New Horse Houghing Husbandry and invented the seed drill.

The truth is that the band's first performances were so inept that they never got a second booking unless they changed their name — from the John Evan Smash to Navy Blue to Ian Anderson's Bag of Blues . . . The first time they earned applause and an immediate second booking they happened to be called Jethro Tull.

Out of the limelight, Anderson is middle-aged in manner and deeply conservative in attitude. He is good Highland mutton dressed as lamb — and he knows it.

The Skye estate is, in fact, Ian Anderson's second home. He already owns a 16th-century farmhouse called Pophleys in Buckinghamshire, only 38 miles from London. It has 500 acres of arable land, given over at the moment to barley and wheat.

Anderson lives there with his wife Shona, the daughter of a wealthy wool manufacturer whose family once owned a small Scottish island off the coast of Argyll, and their two children — James, three, and Gael, one.

Pophleys is the family's main base, but Anderson displays only a mild interest in the farm. "It's beautiful to sit and watch," he says. "But I'm not an English country squire. My major involvement is with farming in Skye."

He hopes to spend more time in Scotland when the house there is ready.

"When I first came here it really felt like coming home," says Anderson. He points out the old timber rotting down in the peat of the streamway near the newly renovated Kilmarie.

Ian Anderson . . . doing a grand job.

"Skye was once a tree-covered jewel in the sea. Now it's just barren rock with a six-inch topsoil. I'll never make a fortune out of Strathaird. My aim is to break even and then . . . gradually . . . squeeze another couple of acres here and a couple of acres there of new grassland out of this wildness, refurbishing and making good."

He has already started a salmon farm in Loch Slapin, but the scheme and the fish are in their infancy.

The one cage is home to 1700 "growers," one-year-old salmon, but by next year Anderson expects to have 20,000 fish in six cages, eventually producing up to 100 tons of "happy fat salmon" every year.

The Skye enterprise seems to be both serious and businesslike. It is not the "back to basics" dream of an ageing hippie.

Here the Laird of Strathaird — whose sole qualification, according to a hostile columnist in the West Highland Free Press, "for laying claim to 15,000 acres of Skye is the fact that he has made a lot of money from playing the flute" — takes a pull on his pipe.

"The most nebulous of my schemes," he says, "is my plan to open a distillery on the estate."

"Mr Anderson is full of grand ideas," comment the crofters of Strathaird. The new Laird, perhaps unexpectedly considering his "pop" background, encourages that "Mister Anderson" title.

"In this sort of environment some of the old traditions should be, I feel, maintained. I'm not here as a pop person. I'm here as the Laird of Strathaird."

reflect a rock 'n' roll lifestyle."

To which Anderson was quoted; "We're neither today's hot news nor a band that can be written off, because I believe that we're at a very invigorating time in the life of Jethro Tull. Let's face it, once you've been up there, as we were in the headlines of a decade or so ago, you can never recapture that position as new bands come along and assume importance among the kids simply because they're fresh, new and energetic. You can only become, in our position, middle-of-the-road *or* carry on in that twilight world in which we exist — that's why we get this mixed reaction from those who come and have to reach a conclusion. People like us or really hate us because they find it very difficult to pinpoint us."

In October 1980, Kentucky's *The Courier Journal* reviewed Tull's Louisville Gardens performance: "When it was first announced that Jethro Tull would be playing in town last night, my first reaction was trying to figure out exactly who would be going to the concert. There's no doubt that Jethro Tull is still a favourite of many rock fans, and there wasn't a question that Louisville Gardens would be filled last night. But for a group that has been around for more than a decade, one wondered if the concert goers would be the original fans or a younger group of new listeners. As it turned out, both were present en masse."

"As I looked around the audience and saw an older friend who listened to Tull albums with me nine years ago, two Durrett High School students, Gary and Mary, were busy to my right "jamming to the music", as she put it. But both age groups seemed to be at the concert mainly to hear the same thing — the older Jethro Tull compositions from the time of *Aqualung* and *Thick As A Brick*. Gary made it a point of saying that he grew up with the likes of Jethro Tull and Uriah Heap, and that he didn't even know the newest songs or that there were massive personnel changes immediately before the new tour and album, entitled *A*. If that was true for many of the people there, I wonder if any were disappointed. No doubt that many of the older tunes were played, as some promotional material promised, but during the hour-and-a-half that I listened before I had to leave to make the paper's deadline, the material was all new, or at best, relatively recent."

"Jethro Tull didn't just play new songs. They played in a style quite different from that of ten, or even five, years ago. And of the new additions, keyboard player and violinist Eddie Jobson brings a baroque touch to the group, having had a heavy hand in the music of U.K., a now-defunct art-rock band. Much of the new music, such as 'Uniform', has more changes in melody and tempo than the older songs like 'Cross-Eyed Mary' or 'Locomotive Breath'. In fact, one listener commented that the band had some touches in common to groups such as Yes. That was especially evident during a long and often tedious keyboard solo by Jobson, which featured an unusual light display involving a giant illuminated "A" that floated above the stage."

"Still, there were enough of the old trademarks to probably keep most of the crowd happy. 'Tull is Tull, after all,' said Gary, in reference to Anderson's noted flute playing, which dominated much of last night's programme. In fact, the performance was enhanced last night as the thirty-three-year-old Anderson, now sporting a short hairstyle, walked about the stage unencumbered — a radio transmitter amplified his wireless flute. And Jobson's electric violin, long his own trademark, has added yet another dimension to Tull's familiar sound. The violin and flute duets during last night's show seemed likc a natural evolution for the band."

The same month, *The Kansas City Star* reviewed a performance that took place at the Municipal Auditorium: "Like everything else, Jethro Tull has changed over the years. Ian Anderson, the driving force behind the group that took its name from an eighteenth-century English agriculturist, has turned in his Dickensian rags for an astronaut's jumpsuit. What used to evoke a scene out of *David Copperfield* now conjures visions of Cape Canaveral. And he finally cut off his long, stringy locks in favour of a more fashionable coiffeur. Other things never change, and Anderson's newest version of Jethro Tull was filled with the same ponderous, bombastic and pugnacious tendencies that Anderson has always preferred."

"Anderson is still one of rock's most flamboyant stage performers. This time he enthralled a crowd of seven-thousand at Municipal Auditorium with his snake-charmer antics, instrumental virtuosity and not-so-subtle wit. At times Anderson looks like a wild symphony director, but others a mad doctor or a revivalist preacher. His use of the flute as lead instrument remains unique after all these years, and the graceful manner in which he pirouettes, feints, dives and leaps around on stage is still a thrill to watch. Anderson hasn't added anything new to his act in years and it should be noted that his former spontaneity is more feigned these days."

August 30, 1980 - SOUNDS Page 12
JETHRO TULL
COMES DOWN TO
EARTH AT £3.99.
JETHRO TULL
The new album
from Jethro Tull.
The HMV Shop Price:
Only £3.99
At all HMV Shops, now.
And at the HMV Shop every week:
The HMV Shop Top Albums up to £2 off list price.
The HMV Shop Top Cassettes at 70p off list price.

"The show was roughly divided into three parts. The band opened with most of the numbers from *A*, the most recent Tull album. The songs aren't as instantly memorable as Anderson's best, and he is writing about different subjects. 'Crossfire' is about the freeing of the hostages in London earlier this year, while 'Working John, Working Joe' concerns labour relations. The middle section was a chance for everyone in the band to show off his instrumental technique, and the final part was a replay of the big Tull hits — 'Bungle In The Jungle', 'Aqualung', 'Locomotive Breath' — when it was known as the top "progressive" band around. Anderson still lives completely in his own musical world, but the newer members of his band have influenced him more than a little. Bassist Dave Pegg, formerly with English folk group Fairport Convention, and regular guitarist Martin Barre, added mandolin harmonies to some of Anderson's folkier sections. Special guest Eddie Jobson added a special touch with his exemplary work on keyboards and especially electric violin. It was the few times when Anderson and Jobson played off one another, such as during 'The Pine Marten's Jig', that Anderson seemed to be enjoying himself."

In November 1980, *Melody Maker* reviewed the performance that took place at London's Royal Albert Hall: "Here is a question that's difficult to resolve for any band with a decent history: When you have a huge catalogue of material, stretching back for twelve years, how do you correctly programme your stage act? The problem is even more complicated with the release of a new album, which the band naturally wants to promote. This, then, was the dilemma facing Ian Anderson, who

JETHRO TULL
WORKING JOHN WORKING JOE
DOUBLE
A
SIDE SINGLE
TAKEN FROM
A
NEW ALBUM
A
ROYAL ALBERT HALL
20/21 NOVEMBER
A
CONCERTS
Chrysalis

brought his revamped line-up to London for two nights last week at the end of a successful American tour."

"He chose to err on the side of fresh material, and in doing so, pawned his long-established reputation for one of the most driving, theatrical acts in rock. Stage dynamics and acrobatics took a back seat to musicality with the new-look Tull. The leering, whirling figure of Anderson was replaced by a bandleader with precious little to say to the audience between songs. Instead, he concentrated on jumping from song to song with an intensity that could have done with some animated light relief of the kind we enjoyed in his old stage act. But musically, there was little to fault in the show. Even though it was dogged by monitor breakdowns and microphone problems, the act careered along at a fair old lick. Eddie Jobson, at twenty-five a veteran keyboardist who has worked with Curved Air, Roxy Music and Frank Zappa, lent a new impetus and kick to all the songs on the new album, which is called *A*, and Eddie's work on electric violin was especially inspired."

"New drummer Mark Craney was rather heavy-handed — not surprising in view of his recent history with American metal bands — and the old faithfuls Martin Barre and Dave Pegg maintained their extremely high standards. There was little to kick against, then, in the texture of the music. The fault lay in the recognisability, or lack of it, in the material. There's a touch of arrogance attached to any performer who assumes the audience has come along totally familiar with his very new album, and the intricacies of all its songs. The harsh truth all artists must face is that the crowd have come partly to see them re-enact their famous repertoire."

"While Anderson relented with oldies like 'Skating Away On The Thin Ice Of The New Day', 'Songs From The Wood' and what seemed a reluctant encore of the great 'Aqualung', he gave complete emphasis to new stuff like 'Black Sunday', 'Crossfire', 'Working John, Working Joe', 'Batteries Not Included' and 'Uniform'. All fine enough, and played with exemplary precision after the US tour, but most of them needing lyrical study by the listener before being swamped with them in concert. And Ian might have explained each song a little before playing it — just like he used to in the old days. As a band, Jethro Tull have received the kiss of life with the arrival of new blood. Nobody wants them to be living in the past. But if the new line-up is to continue, they will have to come to terms more gracefully with a creditable history."

Bells not tolling for Jethro Tull

By Jerry DeMarco
Staff Writer

According to Ian Anderson, rumors of Jethro Tull's death are — for now — greatly exaggerated.

To make that announcement, the colorful, articulate flutist and lead singer of the British rock group conducted a private press conference yesterday with a dozen reporters at New York City's Salisbury Hotel. Anderson wanted to squelch rumors, begun by the band's record company and spread by the British rock newspaper Melody Maker, of Jethro Tull's demise. The group plays Madison Square Garden next Tuesday as part of an American tour.

Anderson hadn't planned the band's recent tour of the States, but he said people at Chrysalis, Tull's record label, "persuaded" him to take the band — sporting a revamped lineup with the departures of Barrie Barlow, John Evan, and David Palmer — on the road to promote its latest LP.

Planned to disband

"In April we had planned to disband Jethro Tull as a recording and touring entity for the time being," Anderson explained, "since all of us in the group had individual projects that we wanted to follow — not necessarily all musical, but domestic as well.

"I've never played with any other musicians. I've only played with the people in Jethro Tull. Although there was no dissatisfaction with that lineup or ill-feeling on a social level between members of the group, I felt that if I was ever going to have a go at getting the input from any other musicians, then I ought to do it now rather than in five years time. I've been saying I would do this for a few years and just never had the time to do it."

Anderson took but a handful of songs he'd written and hooked up with keyboardist Eddie Jobson (of the band U.K.) and L.A. drummer Mark Craney. They were joined in the studio by Tull guitarists Martin Barre and Dave Pegg. The result was an album titled "A," which was originally supposed to be what Anderson mockingly called "the long-awaited Ian Anderson solo album." However, after a few days in the studio, Anderson said, "the music evolved into group music, and it was certainly rock-and-roll." So the LP was released as a Jethro Tull record.

Anderson revealed mixed feelings about "A." "The identity of it has been rather lost," he said quite seriously. "I'd have been more positive about it if it remained an Ian Anderson album. However, it has a bit more thrust to it [as opposed to the last few Tull LP's]. It's more immediate. It's not simple music, but it's more direct and I think it will get across.

"Jethro Tull has become a little bit too structured, classified as a parochially English sort of folky-rocky eclectic group. I think it's time to take a harder edge in our musical direction. A rock band shouldn't be like a symphony, where you have to rehearse a great deal beforehand."

Anderson said the band would perform mostly new material on the tour, with six or seven Tull standards worked into the format. He expressed faith that the band's faithful would accept the new material. "We're survivors in a very competitive business, due to the politeness of our fans, who'll buy one of our new records even if at first they don't like it. They usually allow the music the time to grow on them."

Page 36 SOUNDS April 17, 1982
NEW ALBUM
JETHRO TULL
THE
BROADSWORD
AND · THE · BEAST
CDL 1380
PRODUCED BY PAUL SAMWELL-SMITH
CONCERTS
1982
MAY 13
WEMBLEY ARENA 8 P.M.
MAY 14
EDINBURGH PLAYHOUSE 8 P.M.
MAY 15
NEWCASTLE-UPON-TYNE 7.30 P.M.
MAY 16
BIRMINGHAM N.E.C. ARENA 7.30 P.M.
MAY 17
ST. AUSTELL COLISEUM 7.30 P.M.
MAY 19
INVERNESS ICE RINK 7.30 P.M.
Chrysalis
ALSO AVAILABLE
ON CHROM HIGH QUALITY CASSETTE
IN SPECIAL CASE.

The Broadsword And The Beast

From having released *This Was* in 1968, 1981 was the first year in which Jethro Tull didn't offer a new album. Following a fourteen-month break after the *A* tour, it wasn't until late 1981 that a new line-up of Jethro Tull got back to work in the studio.

To replace Mark Craney who had left after the *A* tour, Gerry Conway — formerly of Cat Stevens' band — was brought in during the recording sessions of 1981 and 1982. In later years, Anderson went on to describe the drummer's playing on *Broadsword* as "rock-solid and lyrical."

Barre and Anderson had known Conway since the days of Jethro Tull's first gigs. During that period, he was a member of a group called Eclection, and Jethro Tull often bumped into them. In 1974, when Barrie Barlow was unable to join Jethro Tull on tour, Conway was considered for the role of temporary replacement drummer. Not only was the band familiar with him, but Anderson thought highly of him as a musician. Due to Conway having other commitments at the time, such a prospect wasn't to be. However, when Jethro Tull found themselves in search of a new drummer following Mark Craney's departure, Conway's availability aligned with the band's requirements, which prompted them to approach him with an invitation to audition.

"We have always considered Gerry to be a tasteful drummer," Anderson said at the time. "He never overplays or indulges in some of the excesses for which drummers can be notorious. He concentrates on the essential part of the drumming and decorates only when there is a real need for it. Gerry has a lot of consideration for the music, and his forte is that of being a musical drummer in that he plays musical phrases on the drums but he doesn't think purely in percussion terms. So that, combined with his ability to play simple straightforward rhythms, and not to get in the way of everything else, makes him an ideal rock drummer."

Having worked together on sessions for other bands over the years, Dave Pegg knew Conway well. Not only that, but their musical roots were similar in the sense that they had both been noted for playing with rock bands that started out in the folk movement. Anderson's awareness of this made him confident that the two musicians together would be an excellent match for Jethro Tull.

Towards the end of 1981, Mark Craney opened up about his departure from Tull. Firstly, he wanted to be based in the States, which, economically, made him an unlikely candidate for any band wishing to record in the UK. Secondly, his decision was based on his own career aspirations. "This whole year has been a kind of climax to my career and my dreams," he said. "I had a piece of a record album and I was in on a first-class rock tour. But it took a guy in a gas station to make me realise it. I wrote him a check and, when he saw my name, he said, 'You're in Jethro Tull. You can't get much bigger than that.' I realised I'd reached my goals. It took me a week to regroup and set myself some new goals. It's a good feeling to reach one set of goals, but it's certainly not the end; I just set some new ones… I want to get a band and start from the ground up. The next step from being a sideman with a big act is to have your own band and build it. Drumming is becoming second nature to me; I want to use my brains and argue with record company executives."

Meanwhile, 1981 saw Jethro Tull recorded several songs (some of which went on to be included as part of the 1988 *20 Years Of Jethro Tull* compilation, and indeed the 1993 *Nightcap* album, and as bonus tracks on the 2005 remastered *Broadsword* CD; more tracks went on to be included in the 2023 fortieth anniversary set of the album). Due to how the line-up hadn't secured a keyboard player by that point, Anderson acquired a collection of analogue synthesisers and accompanying gadgets. There were so many of them that they took up half of the rehearsal studio in his Buckinghamshire home. They served to provide a unique twist to the folk elements in the songs. When Peter-John Vettese — an in-demand session musician — finally joined the band on keyboards, he worked on most of the recording at Maison Rouge studios in Fulham, London (once the sessions came to an end, Anderson sold the studio). Some of the tracks on *Broadsword* maintained Anderson's original keyboard parts, but overall, Vettese's work is present for the most part.

When searching for a new keyboard player, Anderson had it in mind that he needed someone who could quickly fit into the band. The ideal candidate was someone who would bring with them a fundamental classical piano skill set, as well as expertise in synthesiser music — not only that, but an awareness of the advancements in keyboard technology. In addition to this, the person needed to be able to contribute ideas to the group. Luckily for Jethro Tull, Peter Vettese possessed all of the prerequisites that they were looking for.

Born in Scotland, Vettese had started playing the piano at the age of five and had lectured at the Scottish Jazz School. Prior to joining the band, he didn't consider himself to be a Jethro Tull fan, or, in fact, particularly familiar with their music. "I never listened to Jethro Tull," he said. "When I was in secondary school, I was playing table tennis and somebody bought in the *Thick As A Brick* album, and I thought it was much too mature for my taste. They had a piano in this bar. They asked me to play, and I was only too happy to oblige. I could play anything — The Beatles, Neil Sedaka — and somebody asked whether I could play 'The Whistler' from *Songs From The Wood*, and I couldn't play it. I'd never heard it."

Vettese was convinced by a friend to answer an advert placed in *Melody Maker*. Upon learning that the band behind the advert was Jethro Tull, he quickly went and purchased a copy of *A* in order to get up to speed with where the band were at.

Prior to joining Jethro Tull, Vettese was a member of a Scottish band called R.A.F. (an abbreviation of "rich and famous" — neither of which, by his own admission, the band actually was). Anderson said of the new recruit; "He has a flamboyant and oddball personality, but he has quickly become great chums with everyone in the band,

and has very much integrated into the musical, as well as the social, fabric of Jethro Tull."

In later years, Anderson went on to say that the *Broadsword* line-up of the band worked well together. With the group having recorded a minimum of twenty-five songs during the making of the album, it suggests that everyone felt motivated and inspired, so much so that there was talk of releasing *Broadsword* as a double album. Sadly though, Chrysalis rejected the idea, and only ten songs made it onto the album. Most of the eight tracks that went on to be included on just the 2005 remastered release are of a high enough quality to have been included on the original album. In particular, 'Down At The End Of Your Road' is noteworthy for its humorous lyrics.

Just as the band had encountered when working on *Thick As A Brick* (1972), there was new studio technology to be navigated when working on *Broadsword*. Despite this though, there was still the human element of traditional instrumentation including drums, bass and guitar along with flute, mandolin and other acoustic instruments familiar to the band's loyal following.

However, the most significant aspect of *Broadsword* was in how it was the first album on which Tull worked with an outside producer. Prior to that, Anderson had produced everything up to that point. A primary reason for enlisting the help of a producer was that the band sought to share the responsibility of shaping the music to meet the expectations of the public, ensuring that it had a distinct identity that still aligned with Jethro Tull's traditional sound without it becoming repetitive.

Anderson had previously discussed the possibility of bringing in a producer in 1970-1971, but had been advised by a well-known (but unnamed) producer to continue working independently — despite the potential pitfalls of such set-up. Three years prior to working on *Broadsword*, Anderson had once again started the discussion of bringing in a producer, this time with Chrysalis.

Ultimately, former Yardbird, Paul Samwell-Smith — having also produced for Cat Stevens, Carly Simon, Renaissance, and Murray Head — was chosen for the job. However, he wasn't the first person to sit in the producer's chair for *Broadsword*. Anderson explained; "Chrysalis had brought in an American rock and roll producer they thought we should work with — his name escapes me now. He just wanted to get the songs on tape as quickly as possible and then mix it back in America, where we weren't around. After the second week of working with him, we said to the record company, 'Get this guy out of here'. It was just before Christmas, and we were stuck without a producer. So we got out the Yellow Pages and we looked up "record producers", which sounds ridiculous, but it's absolutely true. And we went down the list, and the first name we recognised was Paul Samwell-Smith. Paul came down that night and we started work. And he was great, because he was a really objective guy to have in the studio. At that time I was planning to build my own home studio, and Paul could kind of nursemaid everyone through their parts on the record while I looked over brochures of mixers and made plans for my home studio."

Following the initial setbacks, when Jethro Tull eventually began working with Paul Samwell-Smith, they had fallen behind schedule in having taken the time to find their candidate of choice. However, they found that Samwell-Smith was a great fit for them. As well as possessing excellent technical skills in recording and a solid background as a former professional musician, his working approach was similar to that of the rest of the band.

The delays were such that ultimately, *Broadsword* ended up being released much later than had been initially planned for, with Anderson stating that "we should have had this album done a year ago." However, he maintained that he was "glad we waited and I am glad we found someone who was able to do the right job. It's been a profitable experience for us, and we hope our fans will think it has been worth the wait."

He told *Trouser Press* that he "let Paul Samwell-Smith and the record company have a large hand in the track selection. The final decisions had to be endorsed by me, but I didn't want to be too self-conscious about making an album that was meant to redefine what Jethro Tull had been, and should be, about."

Jethro Tull's fourteenth studio album, *The Broadsword And The Beast*, was released in April 1982. It got to number nineteen in the US, and to number twenty-seven in the UK. The single release of 'Fallen On Hard Times' also saw moderate success, reaching number twenty on the US Billboard Mainstream Rock Tracks Chart.

The Broadsword And The Beast features a combination of the folk-influenced style that the band had embraced in the previous decade — but in conjunction with the popular 1980's synthesiser sound. A satisfying blend of Tull's signature acoustic instrumentation with electronic soundscapes, the more modern elements that were introduced on *Broadsword* would go on to be further developed on the band's subsequent release, *Under Wraps*.

"We tried to recapture a romantic element of fantasy that had been missing for an album or two, without making it too quaint or pixie-like," Anderson told *Trouser Press* in 1982. "It's a happy balance between the various things I've sung about or played over the years."

Such was Anderson's confidence in the music on *Broadsword*, that in the liner notes for the remastered version of the album, he opined that it was some of Jethro Tull's best.

When promoting *Broadsword*, Anderson explained; "There is always that dilemma when you have been playing for a number of years, and you have become recognised for certain stylistic traits and a way of doing things, to give people what they expect musically and lyrically from Jethro Tull without compromising the fact that as a musician, you also have an obligation to yourself not to stand still. So making a new Jethro Tull album is applying yourself to not disappointing your fans, and at the same time, giving them something new, and moving in a new direction."

A strong opening track, 'Beastie' features a memorable folk-oriented melody combined with not only synths, but some powerful guitar soloing from Barre. Thematically, the song is an endearing exploration of the fact that in some regard, everyone is struggling with something. Anderson said of the song; "All of us have some kind of private fear that we don't like to talk about, and this song is about those fears. When I was a boy growing up in Scotland, we called anything that was particularly nasty that we didn't like 'a Beastie'."

'Clasp' features vocoder and sequencers in combination with flute and mandolins. The theme of the song is centred on people who avoid physical contact. It uses the term 'clasp' in reference to a handshake. Delving into the concepts and attitudes surrounding the act of shaking hands, it ponders on whether it would be entertaining and potentially advantageous to approach a stranger and shake their hand in greeting. It touches on how ironically, handshakes are often obligatory actions far removed from their initial purpose, which was for a person to demonstrate that they were without weaponry and extending an open hand as a symbol of peace.

Anderson didn't intend for 'Fallen On Hard Times' to convey any particular political message. Instead, it refers to the sense of disappointment that many individuals experience with all political leaders at some point or another. Whilst the melody is essentially a Scottish folk tune, it incorporates a slightly upbeat rock 'n' roll style, which adds a lighter touch to the song.

Anderson's inspiration for 'Flying Colours' came from observing couples who, experiencing difficulties in their relationships, find pleasure in discussing one another's flaws in a social setting.

Although writing songs that revolve around romantic relationships has never been frequent territory for Anderson, 'Slow Marching Band' tackles the sorrow of separation. Despite the sombre theme, his aim was to keep a glimmer of hope embedded within it. "I hope it contains a hint of optimism!" he said upon *Broadsword*'s release.

With a call to arms, 'Broadsword' (which was also released as a single) transports the listener to a bygone era, invoking imagery of swords and mythology. It creates a haunting atmosphere, utilising the music to narrate a story that seamlessly combines elements of rock and folk genres. The convincing blend serves as strong testament to Jethro Tull's skill and creativity around this time. Not only with *Broadsword* did they reference their folk roots more than they had done on *A*, thus giving fans something that had caught their attention in the seventies, but they brought a whole new range of ideas — melodic, lyrical and stylistic — to the fore.

The sound of war drums immediately alludes to an era of Vikings and pagan warlords who are fiercely defending their homestead. The music has a cinematic quality to it, bringing forth the imminent danger lurking and the heroic spirit of the character willing to fight until their last breath. Adding depth and emotion to the music, Anderson's vocal tone is especially evocative. He said of the track; "Set in historical times, lyrically as well as musically, this song is about a man's responsibility to protect the family unit."

'Pussy Willow' portrays a woman stuck in a mundane and unfulfilling job, daydreaming about a more romantic and idyllic life whilst still confronting the harsh reality of commuting to work each morning.

'Watching Me, Watching You' focuses on the predicament faced by individuals in the public eye, exploring the suffocating sensation of constantly being in the limelight.

Anderson wrote 'Seal Driver' with the intention of it being ambiguous. He said that "it could be about a boat, or it could be about a girl, but since ships and boats are always female, it seems quite a nice fitting sort of analogy".

The final track on *Broadsword*, 'Cheerio' would go on to be used as an encore song in Tull's live performances for years to come.

The album's cover art was created by Iain McCaig, an artist who had been a fan of Jethro Tull for a long time. McCaig and Anderson had several discussions regarding the album's concept, and the artwork was created to reflect it. McCaig, who had a playful approach to his work, intentionally incorporated hidden Easter eggs in the illustration, adding an extra layer of intrigue and points of interest to be discovered.

On the edges of the album's cover art, there is writing in the runic alphabet that was used by J.R.R. Tolkien in *The Hobbit*. The runic text translates to the opening verse of 'Broadsword' ('I see a dark sail on the horizon…'). With an image of Anderson in his mythical-inspired garb as the main focus of the cover, images of the four other band members are located on the corners.

Initially, the band had intended to name the album 'Beastie' after the first track on side one. During production though, they deliberated over whether to call it 'Beastie' or 'Broadsword' — the first track on side two. Eventually, they opted to give each side its own unique title and identity, similar to what had been done with 1971's *Aqualung* (with side one being titled 'Aqualung' and side two being named 'My God'). The end result was an album title that combined both song names to form *The Broadsword And The Beast*. Given that it's the first word of the title, many people commonly refer to Tull's 1982 album simply as *Broadsword*.

Strangely, the heavy metal magazine *Kerrang!*

reviewed the album under the heading of "Tull's Tame Beast": "I've never been able to get to grips with Jethro Tull. All that folk music and what-have-you. So I approached this latest offering from Ian Anderson's mob with more than a little scepticism. An elfin Tull leering malevolently from the cover surrounded by Tolkienesque hieroglyphics didn't exactly do much to allay my fears. But, with former Yardbird, Paul Samwell-Smith, at the production boards (a departure for the normally self-produced Tull), the folk element is played right down and the harder side of the group's music becomes apparent. Nothing on this album could be realistically termed heavy metal, but it slips into a broad-based hard rock niche quite happily."

"'Beastie', the opening track, comes on good and hard and is easily the side's best number. The rest of the songs don't quite match up to the power of this strange ditty to secret fears. With 'Broadsword' Anderson unfolds a "Sword & Sorcery" epic and is duly given the full Cecil B. DeMille production job by Samwell-Smith. This side closes with a silly slice of hokum called 'Cheerio', basically just an excuse to play some flute (and why not?). In between are the romantic 'Pussy Willow' and 'Seal Driver' and the slightly menacing 'Watching Me, Watching You'. I've got no sour words for any of them. They are ignorable, easy-listening or moving, emotional pieces of composition depending on how much attention you are prepared to give. If you're a fan, buy it, it may have some pleasant surprises. If, like me, you're not, borrow it from someone who is. You might be surprised too."

From *Rolling Stone*: "Leave it to Ian Anderson

and Jethro Tull to anoint the eighties with a concept album about the erosion of old values in today's rapidly devolving world. Anderson observes the entropy of spirit that's got individuals and nations in its icy grip, and, with a noble tilt of his head, he unsheathes his Excalibur and stalks off to slay the beast that visits this plague upon the motherland."

"Though it's hard to believe this is happening in 1982, there is something comfortingly antiquarian about *The Broadsword And The Beast*. Anderson often embellishes his morality plays with entrancingly lyrical, flawlessly executed ensemble passages, and 'Clasp' and 'Flying Colours', in particular, have a restless, brooding grace about them. At the same time, there's something disarming going on. The alienation and foreboding of Peter-John Vettese's synthesiser, combined with the heavy-handedness of many of Anderson's lyrics, seem at odds with Jethro Tull's more lissome English folk leanings. Vettese plays very much in the style of his predecessor, Eddie Jobson, sketching a frenetic desolation that mirrors the coldness with which Anderson apparently views the modern world."

"There's nothing wrong with living in the past, perhaps. Indeed, Ian Anderson can make the wisdom of the ages seem preferable to the rootless philandering of the present day. But on *The Broadsword And The Beast*, the real beast may be Anderson's penchant for ponderous sermonising."

From Canada's British Columbian newspaper, *The Province*: "The fresh blood brings Anderson's familiar traits back to life, yet *Broadsword And The Beast* is unmistakably that mixture of minstrel Anderson and

Barre's filigreed electric guitar."

From New York's *Newsday*: "From its title, you would expect Jethro Tull's *Broadsword And The Beast* to be yet another entry in Ian Anderson's continuing invocation of English myth and legend, a sort of rock and roll version of *The Sword And The Sorcerer* or *Excalibur*. And his lyrics still have the same imprecise bulkiness that make you think that he's intentionally writing in some archaic, Anglo-Saxon dialect. But even Jethro Tull must change a little bit with the times, and *Broadsword And The Beast* is the band's most listenable album in years."

"Prominent and appropriately rhythmic use of synthesisers on songs such as 'Clasp', 'Watching Me, Watching You' and 'Beastie' puts the band in step with English dance floor modernists. The change is subtle enough so that long-time admirers may not be offended. Anderson's lyrics still balance the language of myth with topical interests. 'In high-rise city canyons dwells the discontent of ages', he sings in 'Clasp'. A kind of open letter to the leaders of Britain and America, 'Fallen On Hard Times' is a more direct exposition of Anderson's disdain for authority. *The Broadsword And The Beast* doesn't transform Jethro Tull into anything newly appealing. But the fact that it shows any vitality at all is enough to make this long-time doubter at least raise his eyebrows."

From *Billboard*: "Ian Anderson's melodramatic stamp has made Tull albums an AOR staple, but recent revisions in the band itself and the first outside producer in the group's career infuse a new strain of musical breadth here. Anderson's curling melodies and pastoral flute accents are still in ample supply, but a more forceful synthesiser slant, rich vocal harmonies, and tougher, more syncopated drumming all update the sound, as do more contemporary topical hooks ('Fallen On Hard Times' and 'Slow Marching Band').

From *Record Business*: "Jethro Tull march on, and with a new infusion of blood in the form of Peter-John Vettese and Gerry Conway — the latter joining Dave Pegg to reinforce Tull's folk heritage. The music is as expected; songs which begin slowly, building into runs of notes from guitar, keyboards and flute. Paul Samwell-Smith, the group's first producer, has somewhat muted the voice of Ian Anderson but basically kept things straight and simple. The style of presentation may be reminiscent of bygone days, but in the lyrical content, Anderson shows himself far more aware of current problems than his critics would give him credit for. Where he differs from today's doom merchants is that he dresses up his angst in art."

The Tallahassee Democrat made the point that *Broadsword* "doesn't demonstrate that Jethro Tull has anything new to say, nor any new way to say it. But, as it has been for the last few years, the true test of this band will come at the Civic Centre." The paper raised an interesting point, considering that for many fans, the excitement lay in the prospect of hearing the band live — especially because of the opportunity to hear songs from previous albums, which was vital for anyone less interested in the newer releases.

***

For the tour that followed the release of *Broadsword*, the

stage was designed to resemble a pirate ship — a concept which in the liner notes for the remastered CD, Anderson went on to describe as being "very silly." Also, Anderson performed with a life-sized Beastie puppet — with flashing eyes and bones underneath its latex — on his shoulders. It's plausible that the staging and props were not a bad idea overall. However, when looking back at audience expectations of the day, Anderson was mindful that in a post-punk anti-prog rock climate, people might not have been in favour of the splendour of such set-up.

Not only was there a pirate ship, but in full costume and with a giant sword, Anderson cut through ropes for the show's finale. For some of the performances, there was an entire picture frame constructed around the stage, with the ship crashing through it at the end of the show.

Writing for *Kerrang!* in May 1982, veteran journalist Chris Welch (who had reviewed many a Tull gig back in the seventies, both favourably and negatively) reviewed a performance that took place at London's Wembley Arena: "In an age when audiences start rushing down to the front, matches alight, even before the safety curtain has been raised, it's instructive to be reminded how the traditional rock concert is conducted. Jethro Tull reinforced some basic lessons when they returned in triumph to Wembley. Ian Anderson expects the audience to do some work. They have to listen, sometimes to new and unfamiliar material, and to tunes that don't have instant riot appeal. There are slow patches, bits where the folk singing and gentle acoustic guitar is almost soporific. But gradually over two hours the pace hots up, the tension mounts, and you feel you've actually undergone a course of treatment instead of a quick energy fix. And then, as Tull suddenly blast into 'Aqualung', the cumulative pressure unleashes an explosion. Now the audience begin rushing to the front, now they stand up in waves, now they are lighting gas flames, and emitting a roar of delight that drums around the vast walls of the Arena."

"Ian Anderson's boundless energy after a dozen years of touring is quite astonishing. He twirled his flute and pranced a merry Highland fling, and, as he was chased around the stage by a large goose and men in white coats, the old Tull humour seemed just as manic. The band has changed drastically over the past couple of years, and sounded very clipped, precise and vigorous. Gerry Conway eschewed a drum solo, but battered home some satisfying fill-ins, particularly on a trio spot with Dave Pegg on bass and new star keyboard player, kilt-clad Peter-John Vettese. Martin Barre played with the mixture of thunderous energy and restraint that is his forte and was showcased in a long solo short on gimmicks and heavy on blues. Skilled and gifted musical craftsmen, they provided Ian's songs with all the different backdrops they needed, whether it was hard rock on 'Too Old To Rock 'n' Roll: Too Young To Die', or the kind of thirteenth-century madrigal feel that envelopes many of his *Songs From The Wood* and rural ditties."

"Squire Anderson waved a huge broadsword dangerously near Martin's nether extremities during songs from their latest album (*The Broadsword And The Beast*), and punted huge exploding balloons out into the audience. But it was the roar of the band as they got into their heaviest moments that ultimately captivated an audience who seemed evenly mixed between fourteen-year-old novice Tull freaks and silver-haired rock business veterans. With a lot of the earliest Tull material now finally ditched, I thought Ian should have given himself a new vehicle for a flute showcase, but doubtless he has judged that the times are against such instrumental extravagance. Even with these cutbacks, however, Tull have a vast library of music to perform. They could have played on for another two hours and the audience would have been with them, cheering all the way."

In the same month, the *Birmingham Evening Mail* reviewed Jethro Tull's performance at the NEC: "The little girl next to me clapping her hands high in the air could hardly have been born when these songs were released — obviously weaned on dad's favourites. But if Ian Anderson's wide appeal is now spanning generations, his appetite for change appears to have been a casualty. Similarities with the last show I saw four years ago are many. 'Aqualung' to finish and 'Locomotive Breath' for encore, giant hydrogen balloons thrown to the crowd. Yawn. It is still a treat, but the legendary flute solo, it must be said, hasn't changed much in a decade. A thrifty ration of theatrics spice up the lesser-known new numbers and are mildly amusing, but otherwise the tired mad-minstrel antics and the predictable format makes Tull look like some almighty museum piece."

In September 1982, a journalist writing for an American newspaper opined; "The Spectrum wasn't the ideal place for Jethro Tull to perform. This veteran English band managed to draw only enough fans to fill roughly half of the Spectrum's seats, something that would never have happened a decade ago when Jethro Tull was one of the most popular bands in rock. Jethro Tull is the collective name for a group of musicians whose personnel shifts regularly, but it's always led by singer-songwriter Ian Anderson. Tull achieved its greatest success in the early seventies when the albums *Aqualung* and *Thick As A Brick* became FM radio staples. When he was working at full blast, Anderson concocted songs that were bilious amalgamations of hard rock, English folk, eighteenth-century imagery, and modern pessimism."

"These days, there are long stretches of time between Jethro Tull album releases, and it looks as if the band has peaked. Tull's new album, *The Broadsword And The Beast*, surveys the same territory as always, with the addition of a sword and sorcery subplot (to cash in on the *Conan The Barbarian* fad?) and some quicker tempos than the band usually essays (to keep up with the new wave?). The album hasn't fared well on the pop charts so far, and last night's sparse attendance speaks for itself. In any case, *The Broadsword And The Beast* doesn't work, primarily because it lacks the dramatic structure that Anderson prided himself on in earlier Tull albums."

"The band spent the first half of its show last night hammering away at songs from the new album, and after about twenty minutes, they all began to sound the same. The hauling on stage of many props, including a sword that must have been at least nine feet long, didn't help matters any, but the Spectrum fans cheered loyally anyway. As always, the centre of attention in a Jethro Tull show is Anderson, who sings in a lusty growl, dances with many florid hand gestures, and proves definitively that the flute has no place in rock music. Anderson is one of those artists who inspires admiration in his fans by acting arrogant and obsessed — he stares out into the audience with a maniacal glare and whirls himself into a tizzy."

"For this tour, Jethro Tull has turned the stage into a gigantic ship, and Anderson scampered from prow to stern in his tights and leather jerkin looking for all the world like Errol Flynn as a jaded rock star. Once the band finished with its desultory new material, it performed lively versions of its old hits, climaxing with a jangling version of 'Aqualung'. It wasn't enough to rescue the show from its doldrums, however."

In October 1982, *The Central New Jersey Home News* reviewed Jethro Tull's performance at the Brendan Bay Arena; "Since 1968, the band has produced a solid string of competently conceived, professionally executed music, capitalising on a unique sound influenced by the folk music of leader Ian Anderson's childhood Scotland along with a heavy dose of classical music. Among Jethro Tull's standout compositions are 'Aqualung', 'My God', 'Thick As A Brick', 'Too Old To Rock 'n' Roll: Too Young To Die', 'Songs From The Wood', 'Cross-Eyed Mary' and 'Teacher'. Despite the sophistication of the band's music — emphasising Anderson's unique heavy flute style counterpoint, harpsichord-like keyboards, a heavy drumbeat, and guitar or mandolin solos that are as likely to sound like folk as they do like rock — the band always has had a slightly Skid Row image. Offensive lyrics are common in the band's compositions and Anderson's stage persona is that of a wild, slightly mad man, dirty and singing out from the gutter. Yet, in interviews, Anderson proves to be quite a thoughtful musician, committed to his craft and his family. All of which makes it hard to understand exactly what didn't work when the group played at Brendan Byrne Arena on Thursday night."

"It's not that the band was bad, it's more that it didn't shine, didn't really show the uniqueness that is (or can be) Jethro Tull. Rather, the audience was treated to a one-and-a-quarter-hour set that covered all the bases, but was not superlative in any way. Except for a few of its classics, the band didn't even bring the audience to its feet. I think Jethro Tull was trying too hard. Either that, or the band's performance is proof that it is indeed possible to be "too old to rock 'n' roll: too young to die"."

"First of all, the group fell into the special effects trap, a ruse that some groups use, I think, when they are afraid the lyrics will not stand on their own. It's not necessary for Tull, whose lyrics are generally strong and exceedingly visual. Yet several times — notably on 'Beastie' — the most clichéd sorts of effects were used. It's not necessary for Ian Anderson to prance around the stage with a stuffed gargoyle perched on his shoulders to underscore the tune's theme of individuals' hidden unspoken fears. Similarly, on 'Broadsword', Anderson posed with a ten-foot golden sword — the phallic imagery was only too obvious — during a song about protecting the family unit. The Viking ship set seemed useless and the smoke coming out of the ship's dragon face figurehead was merely cute. It's just not necessary and detracts from the music. The band is much stronger when it just plays the music, something that didn't happen frequently enough. Still, there were moments. Almost any time Anderson picked up an acoustic guitar — on 'Thick As A Brick', for example, or 'Clasp', a new song about handshakes and physical contact — the music shined."

"Several times, the group were entirely acoustic — Anderson and Martin Barre on mandolins, and the drummer/percussionist on bongos — and the underlying influences in Tull's music was completely evident. In general, the band played a lot like the way Jethro Tull ought to play. But the show was great only when they stopped trying and just let the music take them. Jethro Tull still works when the band hunkers down and plays its unique brand of folk/rock/classical/electric/acoustic music. When it tries too hard to do anything else, something is missing."

Also in October 1982, *The Charlotte Observer* considered; "Because Ian Anderson has so completely dominated the group throughout its fourteen-year existence, it's easy to forget that Jethro Tull is a band, not a person. But Jethro Tull, a newly revamped rock quintet, left little question about its identity during its concert Wednesday night at the Charlotte Coliseum. Although Anderson — the group singer, flautist and songwriter — captured the spotlight for most of the band's hour-and-forty-minutes on stage, his tight, powerful band provided Anderson's stage theatrics with a stirring musical boost. Only Anderson and guitarist Martin Barre remain from Tull's late sixties and seventies line-ups, but the three new band members played Anderson's quirky songs — old and new — with wit and precision. Barre's slashing guitar solos highlighted selections from recent albums *Stormwatch* and *The Broadsword And The Beast*, and his wailing blues solos highlighted old tunes like 'A New Day Yesterday'."

"Even when he wasn't playing flute, which he did on only about half the songs, Anderson remained the centre of attention. After whirling around the stage like a madman, Anderson stopped and gazed wildly at the crowd of about five-thousand, stroked his flowing reddish-brown beard, and then resumed singing one of his English folk-influenced rock songs. During the band's crisp instrumental workouts, he twirled his flute like a baton or left the stage, only to return with a prop like the ghoulish doll he carried on his shoulders during the vicious 'Beastie'. Throughout the well-paced concert, Anderson relied on visual effects that ranged from his histrionic hand gestures to the ten men in white, who chased him back and forth across the stage while the strobe light flashed. The theatrics obscured Anderson's playing and nasal, gruff singing, which nevertheless stood out on softer folk-tinged tunes like 'Fat Man', 'One Brown Mouse' and 'Too Old To Rock 'n' Roll: Too Young To Die'. Anderson's song selection provided a few pleasant surprises. Instead of relying on his ponderous but popular morality plays like *Thick As A Brick* and *Aqualung* for most of his selections, he chose wisely from both his earliest and most recent material."

***

Following the *Broadsword* tour, Gerry Conway left Jethro Tull. With *A* having been branded as Jethro Tull, Anderson finally went on to work on his solo album, although he retained Vettese on keyboards. Released in 1983, although Anderson's *Walk Into Light* was officially a solo project, it was a highly collaborative effort, with Vettese credited as co-writer on five of the album's ten songs. Still though, *Walk Into Light* afforded Anderson the scope to be free of the expectations that came with releasing new music under the Jethro Tull name.

Walk Into Light is different from Jethro Tull's sound in terms of its moody synthesiser work and little of the standard Anderson flute work. 'Fly By Night' — which was given some radio airplay in the US — is a prime example of this. Although several Jethro Tull songs would go on to be similar in such regard, the fact is that it was noteworthy compared to Anderson's previous work with the band at the time.

"The melody was more to the fore than in a full-scale band," said Anderson. "There's more clutter in a group where you tend to play music that is fairly diluted from what it was originally conceived. As a musician, there's a danger of always working with just one band... You never get to be alone and develop new, fresh ideas."

Throughout the eighties in particular, Anderson's non-Tull endeavours were beneficial to the band. He maintained in multiple interviews across the decade that he was in a position to make music for fun, and that there was no financial pressure on him to have a particular level of monetary reward for it.

Having purchased fifteen-thousand acres of land — the Strathaird Estate on Scotland's island of Skye — in 1978, he remained hands-on in his approach to salmon farming there — to the extent that he was involved with the employment of staff and the health status needs of the fish. A capable businessman, Anderson took full responsibility for the numbers and the land — much to the relief of the locals who took a generally cynical approach towards outsiders who purchased land only to leave it uncared for, not least a rock star! His salmon farming career would continue up until 1994 when he chose to sell the estate to the John Muir Trust, a Scottish charity dedicated to the conservation of wild land.

There's a sense that in every member of Jethro Tull having some time away from the band, creatively, a change was as good as a rest. Anderson said; "All the members of the band decided just over a year ago when we wound up our tour at the end of last year, that it would be a good idea to go and get some fresh influences and fresh ideas by doing bits and pieces on our own. It's the usual solo album syndrome. In this case I came out with a solo project, Dave Pegg the bass player did a solo album, predictably in the folk vein, and Martin the guitar player went off to do some things at home, and we're now in the middle of doing a Jethro Tull album — back with a whole lot of different ideas as a result of doing this."

The "things at home" that Anderson was referring to are that during the break of 1983, Barre built a studio in his country home and began writing songs. The guitarist described the dozen tunes he finished as "pop songs, really simplistic", but would be met with a favourable response upon presenting them to the band.

Pegg recorded his solo album, *The Cocktail Cowboy Goes It Alone*, in his small home studio in Banbury. The cover photo was taken at one of the local pubs. As well as featuring traditional songs and those penned by Pegg, other prominent folk artists wrote material for the album (Ralph McTell penned 'Barnes Morris', whilst Steve Ashley contributed 'The Journeymen'). Additionally, 'Jack Frost And The Hooded Crow' was written by Ian Anderson. To promote the album, Pegg formed a band of local musicians.

Appreciative of the scope to work on his own project, Pegg said; "I've been wanting to do this for ages, but

I've never really had time. Since Jethro Tull appeared at the NEC a year ago, we've done a forty-two date tour of America, which was pretty gruelling, and we've also been to Germany where we headlined with Neil Young. After that, we had to stop for a while, and Ian started working on a solo project, so I was able to get down to this. I love the folk circuit in Britain, because everybody knows everyone else and it's very friendly. It's a nice break from playing huge concert halls."

Whilst promoting *Walk Into Light* to BBC Radio One in November 1983, Anderson gave some clues as to what could be expected of the next Jethro Tull album; "Well, thus far, what the group are doing is like nothing that Jethro Tull has done before — a lot of people will say 'thank goodness'. It is more adventurous musically, more experimental, on the one hand; it also seems to sound more like the present day and the mood that I feel. Going back to the elves and goblins: it's a lot of fun, but it's not really what life's about for me anymore, and nor is it for our audience, I think."

Charles' rock salmon

Prince Charles is breaking his holiday on Thursday to open a new salmon processing and packaging plant in Inverness as a special favour to Ian Anderson, leader of the rock band, Jethro Tull.

Anderson, a major shareholder in Strathaird Ltd which owns the plant, recently gave up part of his holiday to appear in Prince Charles's charity concert in aid of the South Atlantic Fund.

September 15 1984 SOUNDS Page 9
WE'VE GOT JETHRO TULL UNDER WRAPS AT OUR PRICE
ALBUM ONLY £4.49
JETHRO TULL – "UNDER WRAPS"
ALSO AVAILABLE ON CHROME CASSETTE
WHICH INCLUDES FOUR BONUS TRACKS
MUSIC, SERVICE, SELECTION ~ THINK OUR PRICE
COMING SOON: MEATLOAF · VISAGE · U2 · HEAVEN 17 · VANGELIS
OUR PRICE Records
MUSIC VIDEOS NOW AVAILABLE AT SELECTED OUR PRICE SHOPS
ADDRESSES
PHONE 01-937 4174
FOR THE ADDRESS OF YOUR LOCAL OUR PRICE RECORD SHOP

Under Wraps

Following the promotional trail for *Walk Into Light,* was it a case of returning to darkness for Ian Anderson? Not in the slightest, but it was a return to the band and brand that had earnt him a crust since the late sixties.

Jethro Tull's fifteenth studio album, *Under Wraps,* was released in September 1984. It got to number seventy-six in the US and to number eighteen in the UK. It also spawned the single 'Lap Of Luxury', which got to number seventy in the UK.

Under Wraps stands out from earlier Jethro Tull albums because it marks a departure from Anderson being the main songwriter. With the majority of the songs on the album having been co-written with other members of the band, and with Peter-John Vettese taking on a prominent role, it was the first time since *This Was* that Jethro Tull had worked in such manner.

Certainly a collaborative approach, with Anderson relinquishing some of his control, it allowed for Barre and Vettese to contribute significantly. In a Jethro Tull consisting of four band members, each musician had distinct instrumental duties. Anderson took on his customary role as lead vocalist and also played the flute and acoustic guitar. In addition, he was responsible for programming the electronic drums and mastering the Fairlight CMI synthesiser (the latter of which he had already used on *Broadsword*). Vettese handled the keyboard parts and contributed heavily to the electronic programming. Meanwhile, Barre focused solely on playing the electric guitar and Dave Pegg played bass guitar and double bass.

The nine months that the band spent working on *Under Wraps* coincided with the brief period during which Fender were trying to get into the keyboard market. Consequently, the company gifted some instruments and equipment to Vettese as part of their marketing plan.

Thematically inspired by Anderson's fascination with espionage fiction, *Under Wraps* blends trademark vocal intonations with the upbeat, pop music quirks typical of the mid-eighties. The infusion of electronic drumbeats and heavy synth stabs serve to emphasise an embracement of the style, which is further enhanced by the cheerful mood of the music.

Considering that it was working for other once-prog-turned-pop bands — Yes, Genesis, Asia and King Crimson — Jethro Tull's foray into a new sound perhaps wasn't all that farfetched. 1984 was, after all, right at the end of new wave's predominance where electronic and synth-based music was splintering off into a range of new directions. There was new ground to be explored, and really, it could be said that the grandfathers of prog rock were experimenting with new music just as they had done so in their respective seventies' heydays.

By the mid-eighties, even the prog-rockers themselves had perhaps had enough of prog. Anderson said; "Sure, Tull went through a period in about '72/'73 when we were producing heavily arranged, almost symphonic music, but in the end, that wasn't satisfying. So we've concentrated on recording short songs since those overblown days."

That's not to say that the importance of prog and its relevance was being entirely rejected though. "The progressive rock of the seventies is now looked upon as the dark ages of rock 'n' roll," said Anderson. "It's a disservice to a very necessary phase in pop music. It was a time when people were beginning to look out beyond the dominance of black music on pop music. Up until the seventies, there was little around that wasn't derived from the blues and such. Things have changed. I think artists today can put into three-and-a-half minutes what it took ten minutes back then because we were all trying to figure out what we could do."

It would, however, perhaps be unfair to assume that Jethro Tull had decided to slavishly copy what everyone else was doing by the mid-eighties. Anderson told *Sounds*; "I've always been a passionate believer that when people listen to a record for the first time, they really shouldn't have too many ideas… We're not trying to sound modern. I don't like the word, because you can't sound modern if you're my age! I'd rather your reaction was, 'Well, I've only had a couple of listens, I quite like it, I'm gonna have another listen', because it should grow."

Also: "It's progression — the only way you can progress really, which is, I suppose, like a crab; forward but off at a distinct angle. Or a bit like driving down a newly completed housing estate road; you might make a left, go so far, but there's probably some half-completed houses, a bit of room to turn around, and you've got to go back and join the main road again. That's the inevitable face of pop music, the whole cyclic thing, it just happens."

"When we made the album, we set about trying to

combine the benefits of music that originated from what was then new sampling technology with our traditional band approach. It was an unusual combination of musical sounds, some of which were cold and calculating, and others that were more evocative. I enjoyed the album because, as a vocalist, I really stretched myself to the limit in terms of its range and the structure of the melodies."

The absence of a human drummer makes *Under Wraps* a particularly unique Jethro Tull album. All percussion tracks were produced electronically (but for the tour, the band was joined by Doane Perry, who would stay on as a permanent member thereafter). With no drummer, and with its electronic and synthesiser-based sound, *Under Wraps*, which was recorded entirely in Anderson's home studio, significantly divided the opinion of Tull's fanbase at the time and continues to do so to this day.

If it is to be considered that throughout their tenure, Jethro Tull have always been on the outskirts of what has been thought of as fashionable, then with *Under Wraps*, or indeed, any of their albums, they had nothing to lose in choosing to experiment over and above trying to appeal to any particular audience. "Why have we survived? I really couldn't begin to answer that question," said Anderson. "Perhaps we've been very lucky never to have been dubbed teenybop idols. Being ugly does have its advantages. I was once the centrefold in *Jackie*, which must have given all those girls at finishing schools up and down the country a really nasty shock. Can you imagine, having David Cassidy one week, and me the next?! But seriously, once you get dubbed a 'teeny performer' your career is virtually over. No one comes back from that sort of stigma; David Cassidy, Adam Ant, the Bay City

Rollers, they've all suffered as a result."

As the opening track on *Under Wraps*, 'Lap Of Luxury' makes it clear that the album is going to be nothing like *Songs From The Wood* or even *Broadsword*. With MTV and music video having considerable power over the success of many rock bands by that point, it makes absolute sense that Jethro Tull embraced the opportunity to make a video in support of the song's single release. The result has mid-eighties written all over it, with a band suited and booted as they sit in a boardroom and then walk through a corridor with an abundance of paper money flying around. The electronic, precise computerised element of the music is even emphasised in a snippet of footage where a sharply-dressed Anderson walking up some steps has been edited to make every footstep land in precise time with the music's rhythm.

The single was given respectable airplay in the US, with a local station's DJ saying, "Every week it's more obvious: this is indeed the best-sounding and best-received Tull effort in many years."

With a propulsive rhythm, 'Under Wraps #1' is the first of the album's spy themed songs, honing in on the classic James Bond-style set-up of the protagonist sleeping with the enemy, leaving everyone uncertain of who is deceiving who.

Lyrically at least, 'European Legacy' is not too far removed from some of Tull's previous albums: 'Round the castle walls...' The song is about how different cultural influences can combine to result in new ideas.

Embracing the spy theme, 'Later, That Same Evening' features lyrics that craft something of a cinematic experience. With an immersive portrayal of the world of espionage and covert operations, the vivid imagery and storytelling is a prime example of the visualisation that appears throughout *Under Wraps*. For instance, the line 'Hard — it was hard to keep my mind on what she had to sell' alludes to the illicit trade of classified documents, plans, and drawings in relation to industrial or military espionage.

Referring to a hired hand who kills people and destroys "hot" buildings for a fee, 'Saboteur' continues the album's spy theme. It hones in on the psychopathic nature of those who do the job.

The title of 'Radio Free Moscow' is in reference to Radio Free Europe/Radio Liberty, which, at the time, was a non-profit, private corporation. Founded in the US in 1949 for the purpose of broadcasting news and current affairs programming to countries behind the Iron Curtain in Eastern Europe, the goal of these corporations was to promote democratic values and institutions by providing factual information and ideas to citizens living under oppressive regimes.

'Nobody's Car' is reminiscent of a film, evoking a sense of constant surveillance and danger as the lyrics describe being followed by anonymous agents, such as 'Mr No-one at the wheel of Nobody's car' and the 'Black Volga following me'. Volga limousines were popular amongst Soviet Union officials, including diplomats and KGB agents. The presence of this vehicle in the song further reinforces the theme of surveillance and the feeling of being watched by those in positions of power.

'Heat' is a thematic continuation of the previous track.

'Under Wraps #2' is a reprise of 'Under Wraps #1'. It has the same lyrics but with a more organic sound. It stands out as the only acoustic track on the album and offers a warmer, more nuanced expression compared to the predominantly electronic sound of the other songs.

In its reference to "newspaper warriors", the lyrics of 'Baker Street Muse' on *Minstrel In The Gallery* had already made astute observations of the behaviours and influences of the press. *Under Wrap*'s 'Paparazzi' is similar in such nature, albeit worlds away in terms of its instrumentation and overall timbre.

The lyrics of 'Apogee' look down on the Earth from the perspective of those in orbit of it. An apogee is the point in an object's — such as a satellite or the moon — orbit when it is farthest from the Earth.

Notably, with the medium of CD being relatively new to the market, *Under Wraps* was initially released on this format as well as on vinyl. The CD release included four extra tracks: 'Astronomy', 'Tundra', 'Automative Engineering', and 'General Crossing'.

Dave Pegg has gone on to state that the tracks cut from the *Broadsword* sessions would have made a better album. He also said that *Under Wraps* was "designed to make Jethro Tull sound like a band from the eighties. That's something I don't think you can ever do; it comes across as being false."

Although in more recent years Martin Barre has referred to *Under Wraps* as one of his favourite Tull albums, just five years following its release, he would go on to tell a journalist; "The days of *Under Wraps* were an experiment that I don't think really worked from our point of view, or from the fans' point of view. I think that's ably illustrated by the sales. I can't regret doing it. It had several departures from the sort of thing we normally do.

I think it was a necessary part of the ageing of the group."

From *Kerrang!*: "Tull are still a powerful, changing force in rock. They can draw audiences at the drop of a flute, but their sound has been updated, with greater emphasis on keyboards, and the drum machine revolution has not gone unobserved down in Tull Land… On bass is Dave Pegg, and stalwart Martin Barre is on guitar. Between them they have conjured an attractive stew of rhythms and melodies, like 'Later, That Same Evening', which rolls through a succession of intriguing ideas, like a ship's siren suddenly hooting."

"'Under Wraps', the title track, makes a bright opening, and sets the tone for the new Tull, all crisp and digital. But even on jerky songs like 'Nobody's Car', the old face of Tull, bewhiskered and with flute attached, can be observed, overseeing and cueing the sound effects. The touches of flute bring the magic, otherwise one could be forgiven for thinking that this was just another session, rendered uniform by modern technology. 'Radio Free Moscow' is the last and most interesting track on side one; rather than launch into a simple refutation of Eastern bile, the band attempt to balance the picture by suggesting that the Voice Of America may also be involved in Cold War games. The remaining tracks include 'Heat', with speaker-rattling bass drum work, 'Lap Of Luxury', 'Saboteur', 'Astronomy', which sounds like a hit single, and 'Under Wraps #2'."

"The music rattles along with that curiously mournful sound inherited from Ian's folk-influenced vocal style. But gone is the rambling rock 'n' roll of yesteryear and pulsing, metronomic drums now tend to thrust forward in the mix. And for those who fear the guitar may have been sacrificed on the altar of the synthesiser, there are many explosive axe licks to cut a swathe through 'Heat' and 'Luxury'. Despite its marching beat, 'Saboteur' tends to follow the pattern set by the previous cuts and a certain sameness develops, broken only by some rather inhuman double bass drum work. If these drums are, in fact, the work of flesh and bone, then my congratulations to the new drummer, Doane Perry. If the result of electronic circuitry, my compliments to the electrician and his mate. It's all a long way from *Aqualung*, but then so is everything else."

It's interesting that in writing the above review, Chris Welch wasn't sure as to whether the drums on the album were synthesised or human. It just goes to show that it would have been easy for some Tull fans to approach *Under Wraps* with a preconceived idea if upon their first listen to it, they already knew that the drums were synthesised. Notably, Welch mentioned in his opening to the review that he was listening to *Under Wraps* on a cassette tape. Could that be testament to the poor sound quality of the audio technology of the day, or to how convincingly the programmed drums could be perceived as being human by anyone none the wiser? The jury is probably out on that one!

From *Cash Box*: "Jethro Tull is back again, bringing the unusual style of Ian Anderson along with it. This time, however, the emphasis leans more towards current rock, rather than the Renaissance flavour of his earlier works. Though the songs are occasionally wordy and the melodies seem a bit too busy, the tracks spotlighting Jethro Tull's long-time guitarist, Martin Barre, are consistently tight. The single, 'Lap Of Luxury', is already getting some video exposure and should bolster the waxing's potential at both the radio and retail level. Tull's loyal legion of fans won't be disappointed by this latest effort from Anderson."

From *RPM*: "Propelled by vocalist/flautist Ian Anderson, Tull bring their quirky baroque sound into the eighties with a set of tunes revealing Anderson's predictable eclecticism. Key is 'Lap Of Luxury', big-beat synthesiser-laden AOR fodder."

From Utah's *The Signpost*: "Another Tull album? That's right, and it's great. Ian Anderson's lyrics speak of 'Saboteur's as spies, the wealthy, and the 'Paparazzi'. It's not as *Thick As A Brick*, but the new sound is taking Jethro Tull into the nineties. 'Under Wraps #2' takes you back to *Songs From The Wood. Under Wraps* is a must-have album for any Jethro Tull fan."

From New Jersey's *Courier Post*: "With its crisp, straightforward rhythms and more modern instrumental sound, *Under Wraps* does update the Tull sound to a large degree… While less cluttered rhythmic schemes have changed Tull's sound, there are other reasons for the group's sonic retooling. Perhaps none more important than a more democratic system of creative input."

At the time of writing, with the album's fortieth anniversary looming, it will be interesting to see what is done with *Under Wraps*. In particular, not only has Anderson expressed in recent years that he doesn't regret making the album, but that he is interested in replacing the synthesised drum tracks with a human drummer.

***

For the tour to promote *Under Wraps*, Jethro Tull delivered a typically artistic stage production. Similar to what had been done on the *Thick As A Brick* tour, the roadies went on stage, appearing to sweep the floor, counting the audience, and surveying the venue. All band members and their instruments were covered in "wraps", with Anderson dramatically unveiling them to kick off the show.

"We're spending something like £250,000 on pre-production for the show, but it won't be a spectacular effects-orientated staging," said Anderson. "We've always tried to put the emphasis on people rather than one-off effects like lasers. For example, our roadies invariably have three jobs to do, two of which involve dressing up and coming on stage."

Although perhaps rather modest about it, Anderson was under no illusions about where he saw Jethro Tull's relationship with the public. "For ten years we haven't had a manager so we've had to do things ourselves," he said. "Jethro Tull is the archetypal underground group. We've been underground really since 1972. In Britain, we had one number one album in 1969, and after that, we were considered old hat. *Aqualung* sold five million worldwide but only scraped into the top twenty. All of our albums since have scraped into the charts, but that's about it."

Also: "It's moving for us when we play and sell out a concert without any publicity… We can do it without advertising, very quickly. We have that hardcore following of fans. We can do one show at the NEC in Birmingham while Genesis can do five. Poor old Tull can only manage one show at the NEC, but eight-thousand people in

Birmingham on a wet night isn't bad. Everybody gets their shot at fame and greatness, but to maintain it on a regular basis is the province of only a select few."

Despite suffering from vocal discomfort, Anderson disregarded his doctor's advice when choosing to go on tour, ultimately straining his throat while performing the more demanding songs — many of which, by his own admission, were from *Under Wraps*, which he referred to as "performance-testing." "That album became my undoing when it came time to perform it live," he said years after the fact. "I seriously damaged my voice later in 1984 when we toured and I had to sing all of that material every night. My voice has never really quite recovered."

In particular, the performance at Los Angeles' Universal Amphitheatre on 22nd November 1984 was such a struggle for Anderson that the date booked at the same venue for the following day had to be cancelled. When the band took the tour to Australia thereafter for their final dates of the year, more shows had to be rescheduled — or cancelled — for the same reason.

After the tour, Anderson's severe vocal strain resulted in him having to undergo surgery, which saw him needing to take an extended break from singing.

In September 1984 for *Kerrang!*, Chris Welch reviewed a performance that took place at Birmingham's NEC: "Ripping off white sheets draped over their heads, Jethro Tull unveiled their new sound and stage show on their Under Wraps tour. After a brace of gigs further north, Ian Anderson and his ever-youthful crew arrived in Birmingham ready to do battle. And, like all Tull gigs, they boxed clever, building the excitement and tension towards a rocking finale."

"One of the high spots was an astounding duel between new drummer Doane Perry and pianist Peter-John Vettese. The latter revealed himself to be a magnificent technician with a dazzling turn of speed and a real grasp of jazz improvisation. Many a rock keyboard player rambles incoherently or falls back on clichés when presented with solo space. Peter played like a cross between Franz Liszt and Bud Powell, flurries of notes shooting off with meteoric speed across a dynamic barrage from Doane Perry, whose big, fat double bass drum Pearl kit sounded like a battery of Howitzers at the Battle of the Somme. The fans seemed almost overwhelmed by this sudden outburst, and didn't cheer as loudly as they should have done. But then Tull music is meant for listening to, not for extravagant displays of wild exuberance. Ian Anderson talked so quietly between numbers, it was like a chat between friends in a bed-sit, but somehow this gripped the attention far more than shouts of: 'do yer feel awlright?!'."

"Ian, the master flute player, guitarist, singer, composer and honoured band leader of British rock can be proud of his new outfit, which is leavened by vital contributions from stalwarts Martin Barre on lead guitar and Dave Pegg on bass guitar. Martin ripped out some powerful solos as the band worked through 'Under Wraps', 'Later, That Same Evening', 'Nobody's Car' and 'European Legacy'. But while I enjoyed the new songs, the best moment of the night for most discerning Tull fans was when Ian dusted off the old favourite, 'Serenade To A Cuckoo', written by Roland Kirk and featured on Tull's 1968 classic album, *This Was*. And when the band ground out the savage riffs of 'Aqualung' and 'Too Old

To Rock 'n' Roll', the fans surged down to the front, all eight-thousand of them, throwing caution to the wind, headbanging and gesticulating wildly. It was enough to make an old flautist very happy."

In October 1984, New Jersey's *Courier Post* reported; "In concert at The Meadowlands Arena last Saturday night, Anderson was far from lazy, though he has slowed a bit with age. No longer the sinewy whirling dervish of the early years, Anderson is beginning to cultivate a bit of middle-aged spread. But he nonetheless remains a dramatic and compelling on-stage figure and still one of rock's most complete showmen. And while the body may have aged, the voice retains all the power and expression it had during Tull's halcyon days of the late sixties and early seventies. In addition, the band, particularly long-time guitarist Martin Barre, provided a two-hour programme of virtuosity that drove the new material home convincingly while infusing the old standards ('Aqualung', 'Too Young To Rock 'n' Roll') with a tangible vitality."

In November 1984, Wisconsin newspaper *The Capital Times* said; "The Jethro Tull concert at the Coliseum Friday night was an exercise in exuberance. The great British band, led by vocalist/flautist Ian Anderson, played their new and old selections with a great deal of excitement. But neither their musical competence nor futuristic presentation could cover up the fact that Jethro Tull is a band whose time has come and sadly gone. One of the better rock groups of the 1970s, Jethro Tull's group created a very special sound and unusual mixture of English folk melodies with hard rock arrangements made even more surprising by the addition of Anderson's flute.

To most fans and critics, Jethro Tull is synonymous with the musical talent of Ian Anderson. No matter what your tastes might be, it is difficult not to admire the skill of Anderson on flute."

"The evening began with 'Hunting Girl' from their 1977 LP, *Songs From The Wood*, surely their most accomplished album. As Jethro Tull took us through a series of classic hits and gave an unfortunate glimpse of the future (including the dismal title song of the latest LP, *Under Wraps*), it became unpleasantly clear that a nostalgic frame of mind was indispensable for enjoying the concert. Anderson, who has achieved quite a reputation as a stage performer, has aged dramatically. Although he is still a terrific musician, he seems a bit ridiculous jumping around the stage. Anderson is not Mick Jagger. Perhaps it is a hallmark of rock music that yesterday's stars appear out of place regardless of talent in today's concert halls. Even though the evening unquestionably satisfied the crowd, there was a distinct sense of time passing — an idea ironically picked up on by the band themselves in their final song, 'Too Old To Rock 'n' Roll: Too Young To Die'."

Also in November 1984, *The Salt Lake Tribune* reviewed a performance that took place at The Salt Palace: "Two years have elapsed since Jethro Tull went on the road. Once again that amazing group has undertaken a world tour to promote its new album, *Under Wraps*. Wednesday night, The Salt Palace was the site for the group's reappearance here, and it was a disappointingly small crowd of less than five thousand who witnessed yet another manifestation of the genius that is Jethro Tull. The concert opened with a contingent of technicians in white lab coats checking out the assortment of paper-wrapped bundles on stage, scribbling notes on clipboards and knocking over the apparently empty items."

"Suddenly, flautist Ian Anderson, Martin Barre on guitar, drummer Doane Perry, bass guitarist Dave Pegg, and Peter Vettese playing the keyboards, those very good boys ripped their way out of the wrappings, wailing through an instrumental version of 'Locomotive Breath'. The drama of that opening was carried through the entire performance, Anderson's patented showmanship as strong as ever after the hiatus. Manically racing about the stage, waving and twirling his flute as he led the group through a simply excellent show, Ian's wizardry was a highlight."

"Two of the odd-shaped items remained covered for some time, the first being the electric drum kit, which was unveiled for the title cut of the new album. The song was a fine blend of vintage Tull coupled with the sound that has come to characterise the modern music of the eighties. 'Later, That Same Evening', with a double keyboard treatment, made for a fine high-tech feel, and the haunting airiness of the spy story. 'Fly By Night' showed the remarkable growth based on the earlier roots of jazz-influenced rock. The latter song, with a billowing curtain lit by the myriad rainbow patterns, featured the unveiling of the last mystery package. A beautiful woman, dressed in a topless outfit, dashed from the wrappings almost as if in a dream, so surprisingly quickly did that happen."

"While the new material was well received, it was definitely the more familiar pieces that elicited the biggest response. 'Thick As A Brick' featured a moonwalking astronaut planting the Union Jack. He then rips the banner to reveal Old Glory while Anderson played acoustic guitar on that timeless song. 'Passion Play' contained a long bridge, the tremendous keyboard work reminiscent of The Nice's Keith Emerson. 'Living In The Past' came full-blown into the present through Barre's artistic guitar, and my heart soared to hear 'My Sunday Feeling' and 'Serenade To A Cuckoo', Ian Anderson's magical flute sounding exquisite and fresh. 'Aqualung', 'Locomotive Breath' and 'Fat Man' contained a variety of instrumentation — mandolin duets, Anderson on synthesiser, a powerful drum/keyboard duet, and a short solo on the Moog Liberation. Proving his love for the music, Anderson made the encore. 'Too Old To Rock 'n' Roll: Too Young To Die', an animated statement far to the contrary. Everyone was glad Jethro Tull has come out from "under wraps"."

The San Francisco Examiner reported in November 1984; "If he'd been so inclined, Ian Anderson might well have created the first folk rock fusion band. He might, had he extended his concept even further, have even called it Jethro Tull, after the seventeenth-century rural inventor/manufacturer. But alas, it was jazz's loss and pop-rock's gain (I guess) that in about 1969, Anderson and his Jethro Tull electric music ensemble chose to ignore their potential role in jazz history and go the pop-rock route. Listening to Anderson huffing and puffing on his flute last night at The Cow Palace, (about half full) and noting the obvious jazz influences in the playing of guitarist Martin Barre and keyboardist Peter Vettese, I still wondered if perhaps Jethro Tull might get out of its rut if it loosened up (jazz style) on some purely instrumental selections."

"An extended duel interplay between Barre and

Vettese during 'Skating Away' was a highlight of the show; Anderson's flute, once a folky sort of joke, now projects as a firm instrumental expression. His late idol, Rahsaan Roland Kirk, would be proud of his protégé. Otherwise, last night, Jethro Tull was sometimes mighty dull — if loud and stylistic. Anderson, who writes most of Tull's stuff, tends toward predictable patterns in harmony and rhythm; his lyrics, often fascinating in content, have little melodic strength, so the instrumental ensemble churns along heavily behind Anderson's vocals, often threatening to break loose. Barre has been in tow with Anderson for most of the group's history. Keyboardist Vettese is a young newcomer — a potential big number, I'd say."

"'Serenade To A Cuckoo', a Tull golden oldie, seemed a bit lumpier, rhythmically, than I remembered, but the duo mandolins here, the hand symbols there, the occasional bright arrangement ('Under Wraps' was one) and Anderson's witty commentary all through made the show a lively, if over-loud, presentation. The crowd, many of whom seemed old enough to have dug Tull back in the *Aqualung* and *Stand Up* eras, seemed distinctly cultish — they were close in style, looks and response to a Grateful Dead audience. In keeping with Jethro Tull's "under wraps" theme, the stage instruments and seats at showtime were draped with sheets and canvas. As Jethro Tull played the opening number, the wraps were removed and all the stage props and instruments emerged. Jethro Tull is solid, Anderson is eccentric and bright. Their cult following reveres it all — singing and stomping along, even on the selections that go back a dozen years."

A journalist writing for a local newspaper gave

a detailed account of what happened the night that Anderson's vocal struggles became too much: "After Jethro Tull's second song on Thursday night at The Universal Amphitheatre, singer Ian Anderson stepped forward and angrily said, 'I've got a message for you people in the front row who are smoking marijuana'. This wasn't just another expression of his long-time distaste for the drug. 'I've had a real problem with my voice', he continued, waving his finger in the front row fans' faces, 'and I'd appreciate it if you'd put that stuff out *now*. If you don't believe it, *try me*'. Better believe it. In fact, Anderson's severe hoarseness was so bad that he was barely able to sing Thursday, and Tull later cancelled its next two Amphitheatre concerts. Thursday's show did go on, but, vocal problems aside, factors in this performance and in the group's last few albums make one wonder whether Tull must go on."

"Formed sixteen years ago, Tull created a unique sound from elements that included rock, jazz and English folk music. Anderson, with a supple voice, strong songwriting, proficient flute-playing and hopping, minstrel-ish manner, was the chief conduit of this odd mix. Terrific songs like 'Aqualung' and 'Living In The Past' resulted, but about ten years ago, the material began to show a lack of inspiration symbolised by the title of the 1976 album, *Too Old To Rock 'n' Roll: Too Young To Die*. In its last LA appearance two years ago at the sports arena, Tull seemed to realise that its strengths lay in the golden oldies and emphasised them. It was a sprightly, often marvellous performance."

"Thursday's show followed a similar pattern, with only a few new songs and plenty of old ones. The result, however, was often a disjointed drag. Besides lacking much of his vocal range, Anderson didn't seem to have his heart in the phrasing or movements. Just as damaging were some elephantine solo segments, especially one endless keyboard demonstration. Actually, the present quintet sounded fine when not showing off one at a time. The new songs don't offer them much to chew on though, and one twiddled one's thumbs until Tull got back to *Aqualung*-era tunes."

Despite the fact that the band had previously needed to cancel shows, they managed to finish the tour in Australia at the end of the year. Not necessarily to be met with the best of reviews though! In December 1984, *The Sydney Morning Herald* reported; "Jethro Tull has just released a new album titled *Under Wraps*. It was the synthesised title piece which introduced the band's Monday night concert at The Entertainment Centre. The stage was white. All the instruments were covered in white paper. Suddenly, a group of men in white coats, carrying clipboards and pens, entered the scene, supposedly to examine the strange white objects. They ripped away the paper in a flourish of white, and some of the white figures were even kicked to the ground. One was ripped apart to reveal a guitarist. Then out came the drum kit, and then group leader Ian Anderson. Get it? Under wraps? What an amazing concept, you say. Bollocks, I say."

"For some inexplicable reason, Jethro Tull decided that their only Sydney performance would be interspersed with silly gimmickry that was, I assume, meant to be symbolic of something or other. Goodness knows why all the butchers' paper had to be wasted. Why, just when I was floating back into the past with 'Thick As A Brick', did someone dressed as an astronaut appear on stage waving an American flag, which miraculously flipped over to reveal the Australian flag? The meaning behind the sprinting semi-naked girl was also a mystery to me. Female streaking is an outmoded activity. And Anderson serving a tray of drinks to the audience was a bit too much to handle."

"Disregarding the inane party tricks, the music of Jethro Tull has always been distinguished by Anderson's nasal countrified vocals and his innovative use of the flute. As Anderson rambled into the past with 'Living In The Past', the audience responded to his undeniable talent. Unfortunately, Anderson detracted from his performance by racing about (as he did in 1974 and 1977) with the flute wedged in a strategic position: flute as a versatile instrument? The rest of the band, while good, were sometimes a little out of kilter with one another. They were only small mistakes and barely noticeable, but the odd lapse in timing had beat and rhythm occasionally clashing."

"In an era when economy is the catchword, and the three-minute single rules, it was difficult to appreciate Doane Perry's drum solo and Peter Vettese's long keyboard breaks. While other band members took a breather, Perry and Vettese entertained the crowd with inspirational bursts of keyboard and drums, waging a musical tug-of-war. Maybe the most enjoyable part of the concert was Tull's overriding sense of humour. Anderson joked about the age of veteran guitarist Martin Barre and there was laughter when references to the impending comatose state of bass guitarist Dave Pegg was mentioned. But somehow the past failed to co-exist comfortably with the present for Jethro Tull. When the band started into the encore with 'Too Old To Rock 'n' Roll: Too Young To Die', it just about summed up its own position."

In all fairness, Jethro Tull were in a difficult position by the mid-eighties. As one journalist considered, "Shake it up, turn it around or put it upside down. Any way you arrange it, Jethro Tull can't seem to win. It's the kind of problem encountered by many bands fortunate enough to last sixteen years: the inability to shake the past and have newer work accepted. In Jethro Tull's case, its fans have failed to embrace any of the group's most recent music with the same fervour of its mid-seventies heyday with *Thick As A Brick*, *Aqualung* or *War Child*. For instance, the British quintet performed much of its new album *Under Wraps* during two months of touring in Europe, but when it hit American halls, that repertoire had to change."

"I particularly hated to do it," said Martin Barre. "It's always been a true fact: every time we bring out a new album, they like it, but what's most important to them is the old songs. It's disappointing in a way. This year I tricked myself. I thought we could do the whole new album on stage. Of course, I was kidding myself."

In 1990, Strange Fruit records released *Live At Hammersmith '84*. With material sourced from a BBC recording, the album showcases legacy Tull songs as well as several from *Under Wraps* ('Locomotive Breath', 'Hunting Girl', 'Under Wraps #1', 'Later, That Same Evening', 'Pussy Willow', 'Living In The Past' and 'Too Old To Rock 'n' Roll: Too Young To Die'). It serves as an excellent example of what Doane Perry brought to the songs and what they sound like with a more human touch.

***

An instrumental album, *A Classic Case* was recorded in the summer of 1984 at London's CBS Studios. Released in 1985, it got to number ninety-three in the US. It features the London Symphony Orchestra with Anderson, Barre, Pegg and Vettese, with Paul Burgess on drums. Having briefly toured with Tull in 1982, Burgess had returned to 10CC, whom he had originally joined in 1977, but by 1983, the band had split and he was at a loose end. Having collaborated with Jethro Tull from 1968, and having been a full member from 1976 to 1980, David Palmer arranged and conducted the music. The orchestra was recorded first, and then Ian Anderson and the other non-orchestra musicians came in to record their solo parts later. Notably, according to critical response, this approach didn't detract from Palmer's aim of creating "a driving and very "live" account of the well-known songs."

For the album's liner notes, music critic Derek Jewell wrote; "I have never believed, a view shared with Duke [Ellington], that music should be compartmentalised, pigeonholed and categorised. The whole history of music has been one of "fusions" and "crossovers…" How would jazz, for instance, have happened had not the traditions of Europe encountered those of Africa? Compatibility between *musicians* is the key: appreciation of, enjoyment in and sometimes respect for what they are playing and each other. When that happens, as it happened with Duke and the London Philharmonic Orchestra, and has on this album with Palmer, Tull's music and the London Symphony Orchestra, the results are always fascinating

— and it doesn't matter a damn whether the music was originally intended for a symphony orchestra or not. There isn't a popular band anywhere in the world, one might add, whose music more deserves to be given a symphonic treatment other than Jethro Tull's… In their evolution from a jazz-blues band with classical influences into an idiosyncratic rock-jazz-classical-progressive group whose leaning in the last ten years has been increasingly towards folkish lines and English themes, Tull have been knights of the fusion table."

One journalist said of the album, "*A Classic Case* not only shows that a symphony orchestra can swing, but sound good doing so — and that rock songs can sound good being done by a full orchestra, if the basic well-crafted melody is there." Another considered, "Anyone who has listened to the works of Jethro Tull should not be surprised by LSO's undertaking. Move past the strange lyric tales spun by Anderson and his group, and the symphonic arrangements are, and always have been, top quality."

Also, in November 1985, Chrysalis released *Original Masters* — a compilation of material recorded by Jethro Tull between 1969 and 1977. It would be over a year before the fans were presented with a new studio album from the band.

A Classic Case aside, the predominant Jethro Tull hiatus following the Under Wraps tour proved to be fruitful. In particular, Dave Pegg, along with founding member Simon Nicol and long-standing drummer Dave Mattacks, worked on new Fairport Convention material — something that would play a vital role in Tull's next round of touring.

Page 26   SOUNDS   September 12 1987
CASSETTES   COUNTRY   ROCK   CLASSICAL   JAZZ
'CREST OF A KNAVE'
New from Jethro Tull
JETHRO
TULL
CREST OF A KNAVE
OUT NOW
Album and Cassette
£5.49
Compact Disc
£9.99
VISA
All items subject
to availability
WOOLWORTHS
A Great Deal in Entertainment
EASY LISTENING   JAZZ   ROCK
ALBUMS   CASSETTES   COUNTRY

Crest Of A Knave

Jethro Tull's sixteenth studio album, *Crest Of A Knave*, was released in 1987 after a three-year break. It got to number nineteen in the UK and to number thirty-two in the US.

Prior to recording *Crest Of A Knave*, Anderson had dedicated a significant amount of time to the cultivation and management of his salmon farm. "When you're out there making a lot of money and it becomes a big business, you forget some of those basic needs for playing music in the first place," he said. "A couple of years off have been quite useful to me for getting a perspective about music and being able to come back to it with what I think are more essential motivations, and not a business orientation where it's your sole livelihood."

"After taking a break from music and devoting three years to developing my salmon business to the point it's at now, I'm coming back to music with the same sort of feeling I had about it when I first started," he said. "I'm not having to play music to make money to send the kids to school, because I've got something else that does that now. And because I've got other professional things going on the side, I can go out and play at music now — which is what motivated me to do it in the first place… It's really the music that's the hobby for me now, in the sense that I'm now doing it for the kicks I can get out of it; and I don't have to do it as a business. I still have to deal with the business aspects of it, of course, but my prime motivation for playing a concert is the same as the motivation for someone who's coming to that concert — that it's gonna be fun for a couple of hours."

Returning to more of a hard rock sound, *Crest Of A Knave* marked a departure from the electronic style featured on *Under Wraps*. "I don't worry so much about the record having to be successful, and so the music has a lot more improvisation and there is a return to my blues roots," said Anderson. "People see Jethro Tull as a kind of heavy metal folk band, a weird eclectic mixture. The main influence for me has always been the blues, and that is what the music on the new album is all about. There are very few folky elements."

Whether calculated or coincidental, the musical approach that the band embraced for *Crest Of A Knave* was one that paid off. Commercially, the album gave the band a significant boost in terms of radio airplay, appearances in MTV specials, and music videos. "I just think we had an album that was commercially uplifting because it had three radio-friendly tracks," said Anderson. "So we found ourselves back in favour again, with more ready acceptance at radio, first with 'Steel Monkey', then with 'Farm On The Freeway' and 'Jump Start'."

As *Kerrang!* put it, "Jethro Tull, legendary stalwarts of rock, are on the crest of a new wave of excitement. Not so long ago, the band, led by wild man of the flute, Ian Anderson, were dismissed by critics as relics of yesteryear. But now there is a dawning realisation that Tull are still a vital force for great and powerful music. Fans are raving over their new album, *Crest Of A Knave*, which marks a return to old Tull values. Even cynics are admitting it's their best album in years." *Creem* called *Crest Of A Knave* "the group's most commercial-sounding music in ages."

"Jethro Tull is a very strange sort of mixture, and I find it very peculiar that we can get away with doing all of these seemingly contradictory musical styles," said Anderson. "Maybe I'm wrong, but when I'm going from something like 'Serenade To A Cuckoo', which is almost cocktail jazz, to 'Locomotive Breath', which is archetypical riff rock 'n' roll, I sometimes think, 'They can't like all of this, some of this must be turning people off.' Sometimes you wonder if you would be much better off if you restricted yourself to a slightly more limited set of options and concentrated on doing them well. And maybe that's what this album is subconsciously about."

Having needed to take a break from singing, when he came back to it, Anderson's vocal style had changed, and deliberately so. "I pitch everything down in a lower voice and am more casual in the delivery," he explained. "Less long notes, so I can deliver it on stage every night within the restraints of growing old!"

The change in his vocal style resulted in it being compared to that of Dire Straits' Mark Knopfler. Not that this was necessarily problematic. "I'd sooner be influenced by Dire Straits than the Pet Shop Boys!" said Anderson.

Despite having been a member of Jethro Tull since 1984, Doane Perry's drumming was absent from several tracks on the album, and instead drum programming was used. Additionally, Peter-John Vettese was absent from the group. It resulted in Anderson doing the synth programming. Consequently, *Crest Of A Knave* is credited to only Anderson, Martin Barre, and Dave Pegg as members of Jethro Tull (with Doane Perry and Gerry Conway credited as additional members on drums, and with Ric Sanders credited for violin).

Barre recalled the production as being "the album where a lot of things were of my invention. There are still chunks of the music where Ian very much knew what he wanted, but I think my input was far greater on that album than on any other."

"Mostly, it's Martin and me playing the blues," Anderson told *Kerrang!* "There's less keyboards and more guitar and flute. In fact, I played what keyboards there are on the album."

Dave Pegg was candid in expressing his opinion that *Crest Of A Knave* was a step up from *Under Wraps*. "I don't think anyone in the band was too overwhelmed by the last album," he said. "It was too complex for a lot of people. But we're all pleased with the new record and we're delighted other people are picking up on it too."

"This time we recorded everything in a much more relaxed, much more uncomplicated way," said Barre. "I think we've used keyboards a bit too much in recent years, so this time it was good to get back to arrangements that were written around just the guitar and the flute. After being weighted down with complex arrangements on some of our previous albums, the fact that this one is much simpler and straightforward benefits the songs and makes them more immediate and accessible. It's the best album we've done for some time, and I'm enjoying playing more now than ever before."

If it can be said that with Tull's earlier eighties albums it was a case of too many cooks spoil the broth, it's understandable as to why everyone was happy to have Anderson leading the way on *Crest Of A Knave*. "I was very, very selfish about making this one," he admitted. "I really just didn't want anybody else to have any creative input on it at all, other than playing the final parts in the studio. The last few albums involved the other guys quite a lot, in the arranging and in writing bits of music, and I just felt this time that I wanted to get away from having input from other people — not because I thought I could do it better, but just because I wanted to be very selfish about it and take total charge."

"A lot of people have gotten the idea that Jethro Tull has always been Ian Anderson being very dictatorial about things," he said. "But it's not like that — it has been on occasional songs, but very rarely on whole albums. The music has always been very much the product of the people who were in the group at the time, and everyone's opinion has always gotten a fair hearing."

The credits on the back of the album state that it was "recorded just round the corner from the kitchen in the room behind the door which used to be painted white but isn't any more." And that "Martin would like to thank Paul Hamer (Hamer Guitars). Ian and Dave would like to thank almost everybody else."

The songs on *Crest Of A Knave* touch upon a broad range of themes. Lyrically, some of them explore similar themes to those which feature on *Heavy Horses*; old-time nostalgia, countryside romanticism, scepticism towards new technology etc. Musically, however, *Crest Of A Knave* is very much its own. Anderson explained that his approach to making it was one of "wanting to do a more human-sounding record. After having gone a couple of years not doing a record, I wanted to come back with something that fit the bill. We had to concentrate on making very good Jethro Tull records again."

'Steel Monkey' pays homage to the workers who build the urban world. It's a hard rocking, mechanical song that showcases Jethro Tull's heavier sound. There's no flute. Anderson stipulated that this was due to the song being based around a sequencer riff, noting that "it was yet another atypical Jethro Tull song that was a radio hit". The single release of the song got to number eighty-four in the UK. The video in support of the single features the band performing on various sites and levels of industrial scaffolding.

Sounds reviewed the single: "Born too late to have experienced this merry bunch of knaves in any other guise, I felt at liberty to treat these fogies with some of the contempt they undoubtedly don't deserve. 'Steel Monkey' is a not-one-foot-wrong record mixing a slightly urgent (or is it wheezing?) vocal with a neck-climbing fiddly guitar sound and some pernicious percussion. For Phil Collins and fans only."

And so did *Kerrang!*: "Killer cut from Tull's comeback album. Martin Barre's guitar howls as Ian sings with urgent menace a paean of praise to the steel erectors who have created our great and beautiful cities. A towering inferno of a hit."

Anderson referred to 'Farm On The Freeway' as a "typical Tull song". With its ambient opening of soft keyboard, guitar, flute and gentle vocal line, this is very much the case. It tells the story of a farmer who has lost his land through eminent domain and now only has his truck. It is a sardonic but sympathetic addressing of the industrial assault upon rural land.

'Jump Start' switches from a bluesy mood to a hard-rocking one. It's another characteristically Tull song with acoustic guitar and flute.

A mellow rock ballad, lyrically, 'She Said She Was A Dancer' is demonstrative of Jethro Tull's candid approach towards sexuality. Vocally, it is a prime example of why Anderson's approach on *Crest Of A Knave* is comparable to Mark Knopfler's. Released as a single, the song got to number fifty-five in the UK.

'Budapest', which went on to be a popular song on stage, portrays a backstage interaction between the band and a shy female stagehand. A ten-minute mini epic untypical of the band's song length by that time, it features Ric Sanders on violin. Anderson said; "'Budapest' is the kind of song I like to write because it embodies a lot of different nuances which I think are subtly joined together. It sort of moves from classical, to slightly bluesy, to folk, and it just slips between them and you don't see the stitching."

'Mountain Men' depicts scenes from World War II in Africa, and the Falklands War. Anderson draws parallels between the battles of El Alamein in World War II and the conflict in the South Atlantic Island with Argentina in 1982, exploring the anguish possibly experienced by women who were left behind by their husbands.

A simple rocker, 'Raising Steam' closes the album in the same stylistic way that 'Steel Monkey' opened it with.

Crest Of A Knave was released on both LP and CD formats, but the vinyl edition did not include the tracks 'Dogs In The Midwinter' and 'The Waking Edge', both of which were released as B-sides to the singles.

The album's cover was designed by heraldic artist Andrew Stewart Jamieson (but for the single release of 'Steel Monkey', the cover was designed by art director John Pasche).

From *Kerrang!*: "Can this be one of the finest albums Jethro Tull have recorded in years? The consensus is yeah, verily. Always searching for new ideas, always intent on quality, Ian Anderson and his seasoned troupe have been at the forefront of rock music for nearly two decades. And with a thumb extended from the nose in the direction of the arbiters of taste, Tull have maintained their position, prestige and audience of loyal fans. And now new converts to the art of Tull surely follow in the wake of this superb collection of songs."

"Tull have moved away from the keyboard dominance and exploration of new technology, back to their roots. Ian isn't afraid to feature his flute and guitar, while Martin Barre reveals new savagery and power on his lead axe work. 'Steel Monkey', which kicks off the album, has all the Tull characteristics, a dancing beat with shouting interruptions and insidious lyrics. Lovers of the Anderson flute will be delighted to hear it swirling and twirling gently behind 'Farm On The Freeway', a ballad rich in vocal harmonies and images of American agricultural catastrophes. This piece is a good example of Tull's ensemble playing at its most complex and clever. Like miniature concertos, the pieces each have their own life and moods."

"Some detect the influence of Dire Straits on Ian's current vocal style, but in truth, he has been singing this way for years, although there is perhaps more American inflection, on tunes like 'Jump Start' and the relaxed and beautiful 'She Said She Was A Dancer'. This is Tull's twenty-first album for Chrysalis and signals the start of a world tour. The band includes Dave Pegg on bass and Doane Perry on drums. There's a lot of hard work for them too, on the ten-minute opus 'Budapest', with its excellent acoustic guitar and violin interplay. 'Mountain Men' and 'Raising Steam' show how Tull can cook when switched to heavy mode. Welcome back, oh master of the one-legged pogo!"

From *Sounds*: "It's difficult to believe that until now, the legendary Jethro Tull have only released two albums this decade, the last seeing the light of day in 1984. But Ian Anderson has not been idle. The bug-eyed flautist has been keeping watch on an ever-changing pop world and, eager to keep up with the times, he's not let any of fickle old rock music's trends pass him by without first taking frantic and agonisingly detailed notes."

"In some ways, this attention to detail has paid off. The new LP's opening tracks are stunners: 'Steel Monkey' sets a tense keyboard motif against a backdrop of riotous axe soloing, while 'Farm On The Freeway' is a contemporary tale of businessmen sweeping away a humble farmer's livelihood. Best of all, 'Jump Start' hits the jackpot with an old score being settled between the apparently deranged frontman's flute and the pirouetting guitar of Martin Barre."

"In a shrewd move, Ian Anderson has studied the current heavy metal renewal and adapted it to suit his own ends, and the results are impressive to say the least. But in his efforts to stay "hip", the hairy progressive rock guru has fallen prey not just to the influence of modern pop's more inspiring aspects, but also to its foulest evils: the rank odour of Mark Knopfler pervades the remainder of *Crest* like a sulphur cloud sinking down upon a lush expanse of conifers. Shamefully and cruelly, the album is snuffed out. It's a pity, in all seriousness."

From *New Hi-Fi Sound*: "Ian Anderson, the Rip Van Winkle of rock, awakes from his dreams as a Highland laird with a virtually intact replica of the sort of overworked folk/rock that enabled him to retire from any active involvement in the forces of musical progression in the first place. To be fair, *Crest Of A Knave* does contain elements that are new, but they come across as commercial devices — the influence of Mark Knopfler's voice and guitar work are more or less evident, particularly on 'She Said She Was A Dancer', where the similarity to Dire Straits is much too close for comfort. The opening track, 'Steel Monkey', also shows clear signs of direct influences, this time of ZZ Top, although the song manages to survive thanks to some strong hooks."

"The rhythm sections generally are much tougher than on Jethro Tull's earlier work. This is due to the excellent bass playing of Dave Pegg, and the intelligent use of modern drum programs alongside the drumming of Gerry Conway and/or Doane Perry. Anderson's flute work is still a major feature of Tull's sound, and whether it's synthesised or otherwise enhanced, there is no mistaking it: check out particularly 'Jump Start'. As much as *Crest Of A Knave* attempts to be commercially relevant to 1987, I can't see it converting many to the sound of Jethro Tull. But their existing fans should love it."

From Texas newspaper, *The Monitor*: "Jethro Tull has

been around long enough to catch the second wave — as more fans are interested in them as a nostalgia act then as a living, thriving band of the 1980s. Don't think leader Ian Anderson isn't aware of that. Jethro Tull's new album, *Crest Of A Knave*, is a natural for the "classic rock" radio format that mythologises the 1970s, from the title on down. After a few years of searching for its place in a new musical world, Jethro Tull has found a home in the past. Except for a few drum programs, *Crest* wouldn't sound out of place as a follow-up to *Thick As A Brick*. 'Farm On The Freeway' — about a farmer who doesn't know what to do when his land is bought for a superhighway — has the most imaginative arrangement and coherent lyric. But Anderson shouldn't expect too many converts. 'Budapest' provides plenty of ammunition for people who consider Tull pretentious and ridiculous. It's a bad imitation of Mark Knopfler's more atmospheric work — a ten-minute ode to a groupie with the inexplicable lyric, 'she wouldn't make love, but she could make good sandwich'."

From the *Richmond Times Dispatch*: "Ian Anderson's bathrobe has bit the dust. He appears to keep both feet on the ground these days, and a computer drum program occasionally shows its ugly interface, but otherwise, Jethro Tull seems unfazed by the years that have passed it by. Fifteen years have flown since *Thick As A Brick*, the last Tull album that suited the rockers, folkies, highbrows and avant-gardists to combine to form one of pop's most unusual crew of fans. Since then, singer/flautist Anderson, guitarist Martin Barre, and a shifting band of sidemen have wandered musically from barely diluted English folk songs to the fringes of glitter and heavy metal."

"Jethro Tull's new album, *Crest Of A Knave*, promises to refresh that unique listener alliance with seven pungent whiffs of locomotive breath. The lead-off single, 'Steel Monkey', the balladic guitar fantasia, 'Budapest', and topical folk-rockers 'Farm On The Freeway' and 'Mountain Men', pace an effort in which churchy keyboard sororities meet rock guitar shuffles with Anderson's trademark spare-no-tongue flute style and raspy vocal sincerity. No band replicates this sound, and no rock band has the gall or skill to spring as many harmonic surprises as Tull. If only the trash-can drumming didn't break the spell so often. Never mind: *Crest Of A Knave* carries Jethro Tull back to its peak."

***

The tour for *Crest Of A Knave* was called Not Quite The World, More The Here And There. An established musician who had been a member of Ritchie Blackmore's Rainbow and Ozzy Osbourne's solo band, Don Airey was brought in to support Jethro Tull on keyboards.

Dave Pegg played sets with both Tull and opening act Fairport Convention. "Even if Fairport weren't the support band, I'd still be at the venue with Tull from four in the afternoon on," he explained. "All it means is I miss out on my hour-and-a-half of table tennis every night because I have to sound-check with Fairport. It is a bit funny though. I come off from Fairport's set, change, take fifteen minutes to tune up again, and go on with Tull. I feel like I've achieved quite a bit musically by the end of the night."

Although Pegg had been with Jethro Tull since 1979,

he had first joined Fairport Convention in 1969 in time for the group's 1970 album, *Full House*. By 1987 — at least ten studio albums and almost as many tours later — Fairport Convention still hadn't managed to duplicate their British success in America. In 1979, following the death of frontwoman Sandy Denny, the band broke up but continued to regroup each summer for a performance at Oxford's Cropredy festival. After their 1985 concert there, each member of Fairport Convention — by that point, Pegg, Simon Nicol, Dave Mattacks, Ric Sanders and Maartin Allcock — were at a loose end, and so decided to record an album together. The result was *Gladys Leap* and then 1986's *Expletive Delighted!*. Impressed with the band, Anderson invited them to tour with Jethro Tull. According to Pegg, he told them, "It would be great if Fairport could support Tull in America. It's compatible music, definitely English, and it might let you make some friends in America."

Anderson was confident that as a British folk-rock combo, Fairport Convention would prove to be a more appropriate match than many of the bands Tull had previously been paired with on past tours. "It is very difficult for Jethro Tull to find a support group who the audience are not going to be rude to," he explained. "Most of the bands that have played with us over the years have had a hard time, and that's not good for us. The best support group we ever had was a group called Yes, and the best support group that Led Zeppelin ever had was a group called Jethro Tull. The ideal support group is one that's gonna go on and try to steal the show every night, a group that's gonna make the headliners go out there and work. There's been a whole bunch of groups that have been suggested to me that definitely are not right to open for Jethro Tull — it would do them harm and it would do us harm, because the audience would be in a bad mood by the time we went on, and that's not how you want your audience to be."

With a black backdrop displaying the album's crest, and with no major props, the staging was kept simple. "The problem with Jethro Tull is that back when we were known as a production-oriented or theatrical rock group, you could have a telephone ring on stage, put a couple of seats on stage, have someone come on dressed as a rabbit, and that was really theatrical," said Anderson. "In the eighties, to achieve the same kind of performance as far as the audience is concerned, you've got to spend at least one-million dollars on staging alone. There is no point with us trying to compete with Pink Floyd."

There was certainly no shame in keeping things to a smaller scale than before. "It doesn't particularly bother me that we are not as popular a group as we were in the mid-seventies," said Anderson. "When we played New York in the mid-seventies, we could expect to play to fifty-thousand people, and when we play New York this time, we'll probably play to only thirty-thousand people. But thirty-thousand people in New York is still pretty good after twenty years."

"We didn't want to exploit the people by having huge production costs, which would then have to be passed on to ticket prices," said Barre. "We think the music is the most important thing, and I'm sure our fans agree."

"I expect that the new record will do a bit better than the last one, and most people have been saying reasonably nice things about it, but it's just another step along the way — the next one could be right back down again," said Anderson. "Those considerations have ceased to be of major importance to me; I'm far past that stage. The ambitions that I have now exist on a much more personal level — things I want to try and come to grips with as a musician, and things I want to do better. I don't really care about playing ten nights at Madison Square Garden — that sort of thing doesn't matter to me anymore, and anyway we're never gonna do it."

With regards to the plan for the setlist, Anderson said; "We expect to play most of the album when we go on tour, and from the feedback I've had in America from people who filled in a questionnaire I designed, the overwhelming majority saw it as representing the style of music they wanted to hear Jethro Tull play… It gave me some confidence to know Tull's career is on an up."

In search of feedback and constructive criticism, Anderson had arranged to have more than eight-hundred listeners of twelve major album rock radio stations in the US review *Crest Of A Knave* prior to its release. "I took a chance their answers would be very strongly complimentary," he said. "Because then I could thrust that under the nose of our record company and say, 'Look, you guys, if you get behind this one, you have a chance to do well'."

Anderson's tactic of getting people to give feedback on a record prior to its release wasn't a new one. Bon Jovi and Helix had also done the same with their own work. All the same though, the exercise proved to be a worthwhile endeavour, with Anderson recalling that around eighty percent of the listeners polled found *Crest Of A Knave* to be "significantly more enjoyable than the last few Jethro

Tull albums," with seventy-eight percent asserting that the musical style on *Crest* was one that they'd like the band to continue with.

Chrysalis had confidence in *Crest Of A Knave*. Kevin Sutter, senior director of album promotion, told a journalist; "I think Ian had found out what he had surmised all along — that people are most comfortable with what Tull does best. If you think of the records he's done in the last four years, there hasn't been near as much of what people consider the traditional Tull sound."

The *Crest Of A Knave* tour programme ran an exciting competition. With a Jethro Tull crossword that had been "fiendishly compiled by Ian Anderson," it offered fans the chance to win the actual flute that had been used on the *Thick As A Brick* album. The competition details assured participants that the flute had been serviced, cleaned and "subjected to rigorous testing for all likely harmful pathogens." There was promise of the prize being presented to the winner by Anderson himself (providing that they were in the UK — otherwise the flute was to be sent in the post with a personalised letter enclosed). Anyone but a fan of Tull's long-term tenure would have certainly found the puzzle to be a challenge, with the first clue being "Respiratory apparatus for dog-end picker."

There was also a raffle opportunity for those who couldn't manage the crossword. The first prize was another of Anderson's flutes. The second prize on offer was a Hamer Chaparral Dot Bolt-on guitar — autographed by the band and with two humbrucker pickups. Third prize was an autographed set of Tull CDs, and runners-up were to receive copies of *Crest Of A Knave*. All ticket proceeds were donated to the NSPCC.

In November 1987, *Kerrang!* reviewed a performance that took place in Heidelberg, Germany: "From the new album, there's the bouncing bravado of 'Steel Monkey', the guitar-heavy muscle of 'Farm On The Freeway', the tongue-in-cheek epic 'Budapest' and the thundering 'Jump Start'. From the dim and distant past, there's ancient favourites like 'Songs From The Wood,' 'Thick As A Brick,', 'Heavy Horses,' 'Living In The Past,' 'Hunting Girl' and a finale of 'Too Old To Rock 'n' Roll,' 'Aqualung' and 'Locomotive Breath'. And weaved neatly in between, there's solo spots and instrumentals like 'Serenade To A Cuckoo'."

"Like all Tull shows, there's a definite beginning, middle and end, as the band hit hard at the outset with an effective combination of oldies and newies, relax in the midpoint lull that accommodates Don Airey's dramatic keyboard solo, Doane Perry's drum spot and Martin Barre's solo, and then go for the throat (or at least the neckerchief) from 'Too Old To Rock 'n' Roll' onwards; the point at which the previously laid-back audience rush to the front and make like pools winners almost every night, curiously enough."

"Centre stage, Ian Anderson defies the balding and grey-haired signs of old age with an amusingly manic performance peppered with all the familiar gesticulations and witty asides. Acoustic and electric guitars, cymbals, tambourines, flutes — he juggles them all like a maniacal medieval minstrel, being particularly adept on his trusty flute considering his handicap of a deformed little finger which prevents him from reaching top notes. And he acknowledges the applause with humble bows and imaginary forelock tugs."

"There's an infectious sense of fun about Tull these days too (although bassist Dave Pegg seems to enjoy being whipped a little too much during 'Hunting Girl'), and the band certainly hasn't lost its sense of humour. During a short Bach interlude, for example, Anderson, Airey and New Yorker Perry act out a silly sketch involving a scantily-clad female, and for the middle section of 'Jump Start' the band's road crew file onto the stage with cardboard guitars in white coats and sunglasses for some synchronised chorus line headbanging à la Status Quo. Even old gimmicks like the balloons are treated self-mockingly: this time the giant orbs have 'Oh no! Not the balloons again!' daubed across them."

The same month, Rhode Island's *The Anchor* reported; "Tuesday November 17th was a long-awaited night for Providence rockers as merry minstrels Ian Anderson, Dave Pegg and Martin Barre took the stage once again at the Civic Centre. After opening with lengthy Tull classics 'Songs From The Wood' and 'Thick As A Brick', the trio (beefed up with keyboardist Don Airey and drummer Doane Perry) kicked into 'Steel Monkey' and 'Farm On The Freeway' from the latest release, *Crest Of A Knave*. When held up to the light, Jethro Tull's new music, including 'Budapest' and 'Jump Start', shines with their classic sound."

"The band's classic sound, however, was reduced to little more than a tarnished relic as vocalist Anderson had to be washed over with guitar licks by bandmate Martin Barre more than once. But Tull fans were relieved to see that Anderson's fluting and onstage antics were still up to, if not above, par. The strongest part of the performance followed a pointless keyboard and drum solo segment when the band jammed on 'Too Old To Rock 'n' Roll: Too Young To Die', 'Aqualung' and 'Locomotive Breath.' These three tunes seemed to bring it all back together as Anderson, Barre and Pegg shared and exchanged some of the riffs that marked them one of rock and roll's most innovative bands."

In November 1987, Canada's Montreal *Gazette* said; "'Living In The Past.' That's the title of one of the many old hits that Jethro Tull resurrected from their twenty-one-album career to please a compact Forum crowd Friday night. Living in the past is also a good description of this evening of middle-aged rock. Both Jethro Tull and opening act Fairport Convention got their start two decades ago. And though Tull played a lot of their new LP, *Crest Of A Knave*, they kept the long-time fans happy with a steady stream of the early songs that first established Tull as one of the most successful progressive rock bands of the early seventies."

"But Tull have made some concessions to the current rock format. For one thing, band leader Ian Anderson admitted at the beginning of the show that they would be playing shorter versions of the old epics. That's quite a concession from a band that used to top the charts — and thoroughly alienate most rock critics — with concept albums that were often made up of a single continuous piece of music. That said, Tull haven't fundamentally changed their music over the years, and it still sells records — *Crest Of A Knave* is edging into the current top forty."

"All the traditional elements were in place Friday night: Anderson's aggressive flute playing, the usual progressive rock mix of bombastic rocking and melodic bits that are meant to sound like mediaeval British folk music or something, and lots of look-ma-I'm-an-accomplished-musician soloing. The theatrics were provided by lead singer Anderson. He arrived on stage sporting his trademark long overcoat, huge hat, riding boots, and lots of now-greying red hair. That's right, he doesn't look like your average star of this rock video age. And Jethro Tull aren't your run-of-the-mill 1987 rock band either. Seeing Jethro Tull live is like catching a glimpse of a bird of a soon-to-be-extinct species. It may not be exciting to look at it, but at least you have something to tell your grandchildren. That's assuming, of course, that 'Bungle In The Jungle' will carry as much cultural weight a few years down the line."

Also in November 1987, under the heading of "Tull: A Musical Spirit Unspoiled By Age", New Jersey's *The Record* reviewed the band's Brendan Byrne Arena performance; "Dressed in a flowing coat, slouch hat, and boots, Ian Anderson looked as though he would be at home striding through the Scottish moors. But the Brendan Byrne Arena stage was where Anderson, the musical troubadour of Jethro Tull, did his striding last night. And, oh, how Anderson and his band of merry musicians pranced and cavorted about the stage. If one thing was proved at the conclusion of the two-hour performance, it is that Jethro Tull is not too old to rock and roll. In fact, the new kids on the rock block could learn a thing or two from this veteran British band. Jethro Tull has been around for nearly two decades, but the act remains fresh and vital because of the strong presence of personable frontman Anderson and the musical strength of the entire group."

"Anderson — a triple threat on vocals, guitar and flute — gave his all from the moment he hit the stage. His voice has grown a bit gravelly through the years, and the force with which he used to sing has diminished somewhat. The lack of vocal clarity and power was most noticeable on the trio of vintage rockers 'Too Old To Rock 'n' Roll: Too Young To Die', 'Aqualung' and 'Locomotive Breath', which the band used to close the show. But songs such as 'Budapest' and 'Farm On The Freeway' from the band's latest album, *Crest Of A Knave*, revealed new Anderson vocal strong points. These are ballads that demand precise phrasing and control, and Anderson shined in both areas. Anderson also made up for any vocal deficiencies when, taking his trademark stance — standing on one leg, his foot resting on his knee — he put his flute to his lips and let loose with a trill blast on 'Songs From The Wood,' which opened the show, or sent whistling strains through 'Thick As A Brick'."

"Looking at times like a mischievous elf, Anderson seemed to revel in being back on stage after a nearly three-year absence. He reached out physically, effectively using the two ramps that jutted from the stage, to make the audience feel a part of the proceedings. And for those who couldn't get close to the stage, Anderson used his wit. Joking about the band's reputation for lengthy songs, he introduced 'Thick As A Brick' saying that the song had been 'curtailed a bit to make it slightly more sensible'. And noting the band's staying power on the music scene, he referred to 'Heavy Horses' as a song the 'over-thirties in the crowd might remember'."

"But while Anderson may be Jethro Tull's focal point, he knows that he can't do it alone, and he takes special pains to get everyone involved in the act — from the other band members, to the road crew, to the opening act. Jethro Tull sports an outstanding line-up of musicians: guitarist Martin Barre, bassist Dave Pegg, drummer Doane Perry, and keyboard player Don Airey, and each was given his own moment to shine. Anderson also bought out Fairport Convention, the group which opened the concert, to join in on 'Skating Away' (Fairport Convention member Ric Sanders also lent his violin to 'Budapest'). The roadies got into the act when, dressed in white coats and hats, and toting guitars, they joined the band to bring 'Jump Start' to a rousing conclusion. Forming a line across the stage — with Anderson gleefully anchoring the middle — the precision with which they dipped and lifted their guitars would have made the Rockettes proud."

***

Arguably something of a stopgap, released in 1988, the *20 Years Of Jethro Tull* box-set did exactly what it said on the tin, covering the first twenty years of the band. It was issued as five LPs: Radio Archives, Rare Tracks, Flawed Gems, Other Sides Of Tull, and The Essential Tull. Also available was a 3CD and a triple-cassette set, titled *20 Years Of Jethro Tull: The Definitive Collection*. Additionally, a single CD and a double LP album was released — titled *20 Years Of Jethro Tull: Highlights*.

Anderson was keen to stipulate that he wasn't responsible for the record, and that it was the result of others at the record company. His only involvement with the project was during the last three weeks of its production. "I didn't want to get involved with a nostalgic kick, but I must admit, I enjoyed listening to some of the old things. It was good fun," he said.

As well as *Crest Of A Knave* being met with critical acclaim, as the decade was coming to a close, depending on your standpoint, 22nd February 1989 marked one of the most comical, bizarre, or even absurd happenings of Tull's entire tenure. The album unexpectedly won the Grammy for Best Hard Rock/Metal Performance Vocal or Instrumental. It beat the favourite: Metallica's *...And Justice For All*, and the critics' choice: *Nothing's Shocking* by Jane's Addiction.

In itself, winning a Grammy shouldn't be considered detrimental. However, context is everything. 1989 was the first year the Grammys decided to recognise the heavy metal genre. Interestingly, the week before the event took place, Anthony D. Tranfa, writing a preview in *News Pilot,* headlined his feature, "Grammy Awards, as usual, likely to have surprises." Did Tranfa have a premonition?

The Grammys aren't renowned for embracing newer forms of music, but in them doing so, there was a plethora of artists who were ideal candidates to receive the accolade. Bizarrely, acts such as Judas Priest, Anthrax, Guns N' Roses, Megadeth, Slayer and Pantera were not even amongst the nominees for Best Hard Rock/Metal Performance. Artists nominated within the category were Iggy Pop, AC/DC, Jethro Tull, and, more accurately, Jane's Addiction and Metallica.

To everyone's amazement, Tull won. They weren't even in attendance at the ceremony! Anderson recalled; "We were working in my home studio in Buckinghamshire when the phone call came in the middle of the night telling us we'd won. I said: 'Oh, that's nice. I'll tell the others,' and I put the phone down. I never really gave it too much thought. I don't think it really registered with any of us because we were so busy recording."

"The hot ticket was Metallica, in this newly introduced category of Hard Rock/Metal," he said. "I was told by our record company, by the then-head of Chrysalis in the USA, not to bother going, which is a euphemism for: 'We're not going to pay your air fare or get you a hotel, because we don't think you're going to win'. It was assumed that we would not win because we were up against Metallica and Iggy Pop and Jane's Addiction. So we were definitely the odd ones out, because we were more commonly thought of as a folk rock band, certainly not hard rock or heavy metal."

Chrysalis Records' Chris Wright recalled; "1989 was the first year of the Heavy Metal Grammy. Chrysalis Records in America was based in Los Angeles at that time, but I don't think there was one single person in the company who thought, 'Hang on a minute, Jethro Tull might win the Heavy Metal award.' I don't think we were even expecting it to be awarded live on the show… I wasn't personally consulted. In fact, if I had been, I might well have advised them to go. It became a real embarrassment for the company that it wasn't handled better."

Presenters Lita Ford and Alice Cooper accepted the award on Tull's behalf. Cooper remembered; "We went to the Shrine Auditorium for rehearsals that day, and that involved opening an envelope with a dummy card inside, which has a name on it. But it's never the name of the real winner; it just gives you something to read out. I think, during rehearsal, the name on that card was Jethro

Tull, so I read it out. Later that night we're doing the real thing, and we come to this brand new category, Hard Rock/Heavy Metal. I knew that Tull's album, *Crest Of A Knave*, had been nominated, but everybody in that room was certain that Metallica would get the Grammy."

"I opened the envelope," said Cooper, "and when I saw the name, I thought they'd given me the envelope from the rehearsal. I looked at it again, and it did have a different seal on it and details like that. It was the real thing. So I said: 'For the Best Hard Rock/Heavy Metal Grammy… Jethro Tull!' There was a two-minute pause, then everybody broke out laughing. They thought I was doing a joke. I said: 'No, I'm not kidding. Jethro Tull.' There was this huge sort of *Springtime For Hitler* gasp from the audience, because the contenders were really well-known metal acts like Metallica and AC/DC."

"I got to read out the nominations, and then it was Alice that opened the envelope," said Ford. "I was trying not to show any emotion, but it was like, 'What?!'. It was a shock to everybody when Alice read out Jethro Tull's name. Metallica were standing right there, all ready to go on, and they were sure in their heads that they'd got it."

The announcement of Jethro Tull's victory prompted boos from some of the audience seated in the upper balconies. Gradually, some of the artists situated on the lower level also added their voices to the chorus of disapproval. There were certainly a lot of bemused and disappointed people — both in the hall and backstage — complaining and questioning how on earth such a thing could have happened.

Alice Cooper recalled that backstage afterwards, Lita Ford still thought he had done it as a joke. He had to show her the card as proof that he hadn't! After the initial disbelief, it seemed that everyone was able to laugh it off as it was undoubtedly the funniest thing that had happened at the show that evening. Cooper couldn't help but make a quip to Metallica, saying to them, "You know, if you got a little heavier, you could be up there with Jethro Tull."

Following the ceremony, the majority of critics were pretty much unanimous in their lambasting of the National Academy of Recording Arts and Sciences for their selection of Tull over newer and younger artists who were deemed to be better representations of the late eighties metal explosion. Many voices echoed the sentiment that Tull, a band widely known for their fusion of folk, blues, and rock primarily featured on classic rock radio, did not even merit a nomination, let alone the award. In the media uproar that followed, *Entertainment Weekly* named Jethro Tull's award the biggest upset in Grammy history.

"It's lucky I didn't go, really," said Anderson. "There's no way I could have accepted it under those circumstances. I'd have had to give it back or something. That would've caused a bit of a stir."

However, he later reflected, "The poor unfortunate Alice was hailed by a torrent of abuse and boos and whistles and cat-calls, because the audience was pissed off that their darlings, Metallica, hadn't won. It made me a bit angry that Alice had to face that negative and nasty reaction. Actually, if I had been there, I'd have loved it. If they had been booing and screeching at me, it would have been such a fantastic moment for a one-line put-down."

The reality of the situation was that the guys in the

Grammy organisation, as pointed out by Metallica's Danish drummer Lars Ulrich, were generally of an age where they didn't recognise any of the names except Jethro Tull. Alice Cooper was of the belief that he didn't think they'd even heard of Metallica, who were a pretty new band. Everybody who was in touch with modern rock knew who they were, but the vote was made by a different crowd. Ulrich seemed particularly peeved: "Let's face it, they really fucked up. Jethro Tull getting Best Hard Rock/Heavy Metal Recording? I mean, come on!"

Ulrich recalled; "Some three weeks before the awards, all those who are "in touch" — the critics, the day-to-day involved people — assumed that Metallica would walk away with the award. It's easy for the in-touch people to think that, but remember that most of the academy, who vote for the nominees, are in the age group of forty to sixty, and are very much less in tune with what goes on in the music scene."

"Obviously, we were pleased to have won," said Anderson. "But we didn't really start thinking about it until a couple of days later when the news started to filter out about how badly the award had been received in Los Angeles. I think one New York paper even referred to us as 'the now-defunct Jethro Tull'. Tongue in cheek, our record company placed the *Billboard* ad with the strapline. When the Grammy trophies finally arrived, one of them, I think it was Martin Barre's, had actually got broken in transit."

And what a strapline it was! Maintaining a sense of humour on the outcome, and not ones to miss an opportunity, Chrysalis promoted Jethro Tull in the music press with a graphic stating that "The flute is a heavy, metal instrument!".

Years later, Anderson mischievously commented; "There was a widespread rumour that Metallica had printed up several-thousand T-shirts saying 'Metallica — Grammy Winners', which are now probably quite valuable if you can lay hands on one."

In all seriousness though, at the time, Anderson went on to tell a journalist, "It does actually mean something to me. There are no gold albums hanging on my wall, no photographs or press clippings. I've never kept anything, any memorabilia or sort of little emblems of success. I've given them away or my mother has them. But the Grammy, it is sitting in the house."

It's understandable as to how the Grammy awarded to *Crest Of A Knave* was controversial. It did, after all, prompt many to dispute whether the album — or indeed Jethro Tull — could be classified as hard rock or heavy metal. On the harder end of the spectrum, it's plausible that Barre's guitar work went quite some way towards informing the heavy metal tag that some chose to put on *Crest Of A Knave*. It's no secret that when Anderson wrote and produced the album, he designed it to showcase Barre's talents. "The songs were constructed to allow the guitar playing to come through, and to create the best possible framework to let Martin do his best," he said.

Notably though, Barre probably didn't think of himself as a heavy metal musician. He told a journalist in 1984; "Heavy metal bands? There's nothing to listen to. There's nothing wrong with it, it's got a lot of life in it. Whatever. Live and let live. There's no future for me at my age in heavy metal." As part of this, the guitarist added that he wanted to "look towards jazz, jazz techniques and jazz knowledge to improve my playing. Because I was brought up on rock and roll and blues, I would always use that."

Chris Wright considered; *"Crest Of A Knave*, obviously, wasn't a heavy metal record. There are very few Jethro Tull tracks that could ever even vaguely fit that description. Something like 'Locomotive Breath' might be considered a heavy rock track, but you would never describe them as a heavy metal act."

Anderson considered that the award was given as more of a nod to the band overall, rather than for *Crest Of A Knave* specifically: "I must admit it, I was surprised when I heard that we'd been nominated in that category. But then I heard that the people who vote are six-thousand industry people, writers, musicians, recording engineers — my peer group, really. People who've been in the industry as long as we have. Then it made sense… When we did win, I thought that it's not because of one particular album, but more for twenty years of Jethro Tull being around. They must've thought, 'They're not such bad guys after all, so give 'em a Grammy!'. The fact that it was in the metal category, really, really pissed off some members of the press because they thought we shouldn't even have been nominated. And when we actually won, they really got their knickers in a twist. However, we won it, Metallica didn't, and they may or may not live to fight another day. The other argument, of course, is if Metallica stay around for twenty years, then they may pick one up… My own view is that it's just a bit of American fun. I can't see why people should get so upset at us. As if it's our fault we won!"

The following year, more suitable acts were nominated (Dokken, Queensrÿche), and Metallica won. At that ceremony, Milli Vanilli won Best New Artist, an award they had to give back when it was revealed that they didn't even sing on their album. To many, Tull's award in 1989 was arguably just as contentious, but clearly for different reasons.

As a result of the Tull controversy, in 1990, NARAS split the genres into two separate awards, creating categories for Best Hard Rock Performance, and Best Metal Performance. Metallica immediately won in the latter category. In 1992, when Metallica won the Grammy for Best Heavy Metal album for their 1991 self-titled release, during the band's acceptance speech, Lars Ulrich said, "We would personally like to thank Jethro Tull for not releasing an album this year!" (Jethro Tull actually released *Catfish Rising* in 1991, but still.)

Decades later, perhaps the final word on this melodrama should come from Anderson himself. During an interview with Meltdown of Detroit's WRIF radio station that was broadcast on 4th May 2023, upon being asked where he keeps his Grammy, he said; "Well, my son actually found it a few years ago. It disappeared for about twenty years, and he stumbled upon it. He came down and said, 'What is this?', and I said, 'That's the Grammy. Where did you find that?' And he said, 'Oh, it was in one of the bedrooms upstairs, in a cupboard somewhere.' And I said, 'Well, there you go.' And since I have not seen it advertised on eBay, I must assume that he actually returned it to the cupboard that it came from. But I haven't seen it again since. I haven't gone looking for it."

"I am not disparaging or negative about peer-group accolades. It's very nice to have people enjoy your work, especially when it's the five-thousand voting members of the National Academy of Recording Arts and Sciences. But it's not something that I want to revel in. I am not a trophy-hunter. You don't find Grammys in my house displayed, or gold albums on the wall, or the head of a moose that I have shot with a large-calibre rifle. I'm just not that kind of a guy. I don't do trophies."

JETHRO STAR ON THE HOOK!

By GORDON AIRS

MILLIONAIRE Ian Anderson of rock band Jethro Tull was under attack yesterday.

For the Scots-born star has been given a £141,000 handout to expand his smoked salmon business.

The cash comes from the Highland and Islands Development Board.

And the move has been slammed by councillors and by an animal rights group.

Anderson, 40, bought the Strathaird Estate on Skye in 1978. He employs more than 40 on island fish farms and another 35 at his smoked salmon factory in Inverness.

The handout will help with his £700,000 expansion plans which will mean an extra 25 full-time workers and another five seasonal.

Highland regional councillor Dan Corbett said: "I would rather see the money going to a chap starting off, but it is a compromise."

Fort William councillor Dr Mike Foxley said: "I am slightly bemused by the amount of money being handed out to the fish farming industry."

KILLING

And an Animal Concern Scotland spokesman said: "It's ridiculous. Instead of him getting this public money there should be a stop on it.

"He is part of a Scottish fish farm industry that has got out of control.

"The Marine Conservation Society estimate that fish farmers are killing 1000 seals a year to protect their salmon stocks – we reckon it is double that."

Ian Anderson began the 1980s with hopes
of making his first solo album. However,
pressure from Chrysalis resulted in the album
being branded under the Jethro Tull name – a
more commercially viable identity.
(Goddard Archive / Alamy Stock Photo)

A selection of photos taken at Oxford Airport in July 1980 for the promotion of *A*.
(Goddard Archive / Alamy Stock Photo)

ARTMENT

Tull entered the 1980s still able to command the big stage. Madison Square Garden, 9th October 1980.

(Bill O'Leary / Timeless Concert Images)

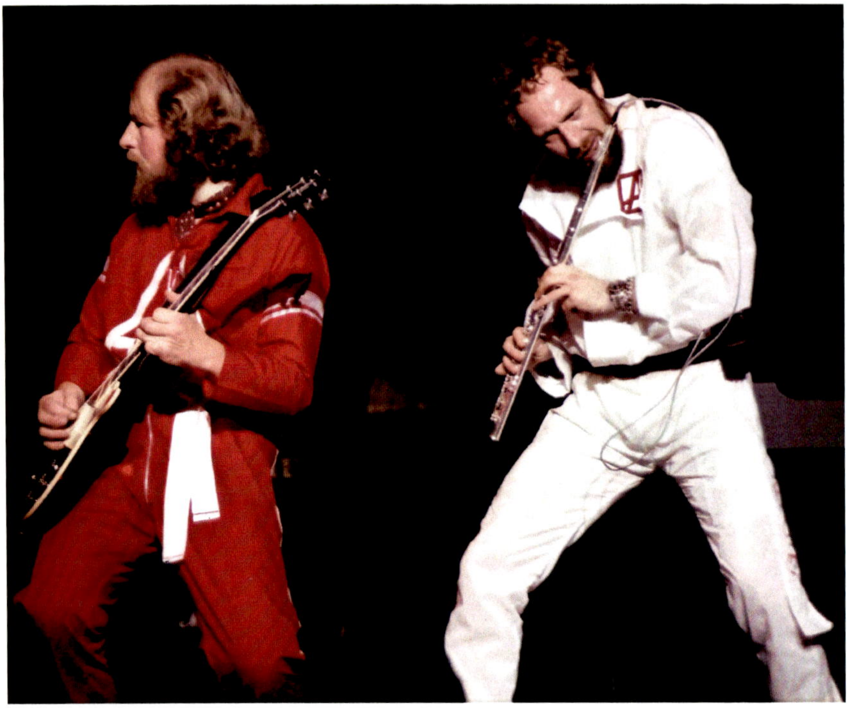

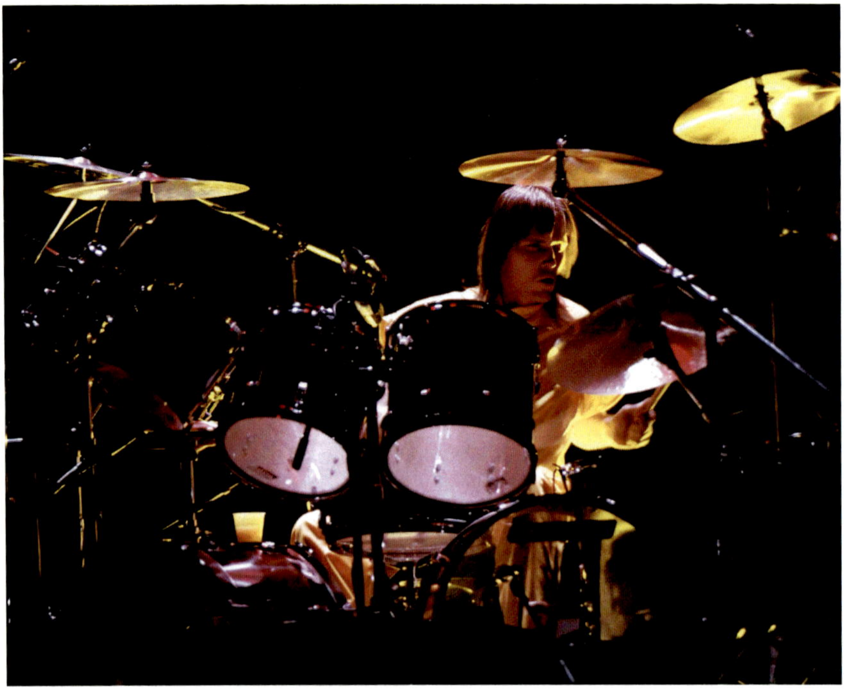

Martin Barre on the last date of the A tour at the Royal Albert Hall, London, 21st November 1980.

(Odile Noël / Lebrecht Music & Arts / Alamy Stock Photo)

Ian Anderson on the last date of the A tour
at the Royal Albert Hall, London,
21st November 1980.

(Odile Noël / Lebrecht Music & Arts / Alamy Stock Photo)

Dave Pegg at the Royal Albert Hall,
London, 21st November 1980.
(Odile Noël / Lebrecht Music & Arts / Alamy Stock Photo)

Promoting
*The Broadsword And
The Beast*
on German TV, 1982.
(*United Archives GmbH / Alamy
Stock Photo*)

Ian Anderson backstage at the Theakston Festival at Nostel Priory, Wakefield, 28th August 1982.
(Goddard Archive / Alamy Stock Photo)

Ian Anderson happy to play saxophone in a cornfield as part of the promotion for 1984's *Under Wraps*.

(Goddard Archive / Alamy Stock Photo)

A new line-up for September 1987. Ian Anderson and former Rainbow keyboard player Don Airey are in focus, unlike Martin Barre, Dave Pegg and Doane Perry.

(Goddard Archive / Alamy Stock Photo)

All are in focus here, but this short-lived line-up only did one tour from October through to December.

Rock Island

Even though the incredulous reaction to Jethro Tull's Grammy success would linger and continue to be talked about years later, the band continued to do what they knew best. In August 1989, they released *Rock Island* — their seventeenth studio album. It got to number eighteen in the UK and to number fifty-six in the US.

Even for the album's press release, Anderson was candid about where he saw Jethro Tull in comparison to other groups. "I think that if Jethro Tull were a young unknown band looking for a record deal today, we wouldn't get out of the starting blocks," he explained. "We'd be considered far too eclectic, and we'd probably be unwilling to do the silly things you have to do in order to become successful. I think we benefited from coming of age during a period when bands were allowed the space to carve out their own territory, and that's one of the things that's made it possible for us to carry on."

The *Rock Island* line-up was Ian Anderson, Martin Barre, Dave Pegg, and Doane Perry. Although Perry had been a member of the band since 1984, *Rock Island* was his first complete recording with the group. Without a permanent keyboard player in the line-up, Fairport Convention's Maartin Allcock and former Tull member Peter Vettese took turns in filling in for the role.

Recorded at Anderson's home studio and with him on

songwriting and production duties, *Rock Island* continued in the hard rock direction that the band had utilised on *Crest Of A Knave.* "I think this record basically continues the direction of *Crest Of A Knave*," Anderson said when promoting it. "We tried to stick more to our basic blues and rock 'n' roll influences and tried to stay away from the more folky or classical stuff. Another thing I set out to do on this one was to capture live-sounding instrumental textures, trying to get the instruments to sound like they were meant to sound, rather than using them to trigger other sounds."

Vitally though, *Rock Island* was still designed to be unique in its own way, with some of the similarities to *Crest Of A Knave* perhaps being more the product of coincidence. "I don't think the songs really have any throwback to *Crest Of A Knave*," said Barre. "The structure of working on the album was the same, in as much as Ian, Dave and I working closely together in the studio. I think that's because the keyboards are structured the same way. We aimed for the same sort of space in the music for guitar and flute to really come through."

Tull's signature blend of blues-based rock, R&B, and classical influences are highly present throughout the album. Anderson's flute, which was not prominent on *Crest Of A Knave*, adds a pleasant touch to the varied songs that range from introspective personal accounts to global themes.

Despite the number of catchy rock numbers on the album, Anderson acknowledged that *Rock Island* is less upbeat in mood than *Crest Of A Knave.* "This was another instance in which we released a dark album after a bright-sounding, upbeat album," he said. "*Rock Island* didn't produce a lot of classic-sounding Jethro Tull songs, but it does have a lot of idiosyncratic Jethro Tull-sounding songs. It's just a more sombre album, and I guess you have to be in the right mood to listen to it. Like if your granny's just died or the dog got run over, you might put this album on to make you feel even worse."

Although *Rock Island* explores a range of themes and ideas, with illustrations by Jim Gibson, the cover extends upon the nautical theme that features on the album. Despite the turbulence of the waves in the deep sea, a hand is defiantly holding up a flute above the water.

The majority of the songs on *Rock Island* were written quickly. "I wrote eight of the ten songs during a ten-day period," said Anderson.

'Kissing Willie' takes a rather obvious approach to exploring love and life within the dreary confines of factory walls. It was inspired by a story from Pegg — either real or imagined — about an uncomfortable fumbling encounter between two people behind the gasworks on the outskirts of his hometown of Birmingham.

A video was made to support the single release of the song. Anderson went on in later years to express regret for its over-the-top style, stating that it wasn't "one of my proudest moments." The director, Storm Thorgerson, wanted to go for a double-entendre oriented, Benny Hill-style of humour. With such style of humour being regarded as quite dated by the late eighties, the video failed to garner airplay. Still though, a hit on rock radio, 'Kissing Willie' got to number six on the US Mainstream Rock Chart.

Kerrang! said of the song; "A bawdy tale of oral sex in a market town, it's the latest in a long-ish line of examples of Anderson's rampant schoolboy humour. It's a part of the Anderson enigma. As seriously as he still takes Tull, such silly songs, in one-per-album moderation, appeal to him."

According to Martin Barre, none of the songs on *Rock Island* were written with the intention of them being a single. "I don't particularly think there is a single on the album as such," he told a journalist on the year of the album's release. "There's not a track that was aimed at being a single. We're not a top-twenty band. We never really were. We're not now. We'd find it very difficult to be in a position where you have to write a single, and then another one and then another one. It's a dangerous area to be in because it's got so much to do with fashion. There's so many singles bands and they won't last, partly because people move on to something else. They're kind of consumer products that get used and left behind."

A moderately paced rocker in the style of ZZ Top, Anderson described the funky and guitar-based 'The Rattlesnake Trail' as simply "an excuse for a funky rocking good time."

'Ears Of Tin' explores the breakdown of social cohesion in the West Highlands of Scotland, where people were leaving for urban areas. The song delves into the feelings of remorse and nostalgia that often accompany such departures.

'Undressed To Kill' offers a glimpse into the life of a working girl at a strip club. The lyrics capture the essence of the young woman's personality, revealing a sense of melancholy and gritty determination that exists beneath the surface of the seemingly frivolous lap dance setting.

A well-crafted song, the album's title track

effectively conveys feelings of isolation, detachment, and apprehension towards the unknown. The rock island is used as a metaphor for the secluded yet recognisable state of mind that everyone tends to retreat to from time to time — a safe haven. As Anderson likened it to in later years, "the blue baby blanket security. Back to the womb. For beer, curry and a game of skittles."

'Heavy Water' highlights the devastating environmental impact of the Chernobyl disaster, whilst also drawing inspiration from the harsh reality of industrial pollution and acid rain. The lyrics are informed by Anderson's personal recollection of a particularly hot and humid summer in early 1970s New York City, where raindrops falling on his sleeve were disconcertingly black in colour, a testament to the effects of pollution.

Anderson has gone on to say that 'Another Christmas Song' is "probably my favourite piece from the album, being generally uplifting in this sea of misery!" A song featuring themes of family unity, nostalgia, and kindness, he wrote it as a follow-up to 'Christmas Song' (the B-side on the 1968 single, 'Love Story'). Released as a single in 1989, 'Another Christmas Song' got to number ninety-five in the UK.

'The Whaler's Dues' broaches the sensitive topic of whale hunting from the viewpoint of a sailor aboard a whaling vessel. The song is set in modern times and doesn't attempt to justify or defend the practice, but rather places the protagonist — whether a hero or villain — on trial for their actions. The song invites listeners to reflect on the moral implications of whaling.

'Big Riff And Mando' was inspired by a real-life incident that occurred a few months prior to its creation, involving the theft of Martin Barre's mandolin from backstage after a show in the US. Understandably devastated by the loss, Barre and the band made a public appeal through a local classic rock radio station to the individual responsible for the theft. To everyone's surprise, the mandolin was eventually returned undamaged. "Why did the thief take it?" Anderson mused in later years. "To brag out? To have as a souvenir? Or to keep for a few years until Ebay was invented? Marty is Martin, obviously. Big Riff is the imagined thief and a little story is invented here to portray the character and his motives." The song also reflects on what it is to be on the road.

A return to the *Aqualung* setting of 1971, 'Strange Avenues' explores similar themes. It features a well-crafted musical arrangement and plenty of dramatic elements. "Sometimes it is so nice to revisit an earlier song and re-create, for a moment, the subject in another piece of invaded personal space," said Anderson.

Jerry Ewing reviewed *Rock Island* for *Metal Forces*: "It most certainly is a lot more rock orientated than its predecessor *Crest Of A Knave*, and from the off-set, it's the guitars of Martin Barre that come to the fore. Ian Anderson's gruff yet rustic vocals are still one of Jethro Tull's main attractions, and his flute weaves its way in and out of the material in an intriguing manner. The likes of 'Kissing Willie', 'Rock Island', 'Big Riff And Mando' and 'The Rattlesnake Trail' are all good, solid hard rock songs that rock harder than Tull have done in the past, yet the wonderful 'Another Christmas Story' and 'The Whaler's Dues' prove that the band have lost none of that rustic charm that has endeared them to so many in the past."

"It has to be said that this album is unlikely to win the band over to many new fans, and will probably go largely ignored by the British media, despite its class. It does prove that Jethro Tull is still very much an ongoing hard rock concern that have largely stuck to their roots and continue to enjoy themselves whilst making music. As elder statesmen of the British rock fraternity, Jethro Tull do this country proud and provide a shining example that far too many people are too willing to ignore. Whilst they continue to make quality music such as this, I for one am going to support the band, despite what other people say about them, and even if I do have to stand on one leg wearing a codpiece!"

From *Sounds*: "The biggest codpieces, the tuffest Highland warrior regalia — the Tull 'ad the lot. But are they really the 'eaviest? *Rock Island* opens with a tussle-haired, firm-buttocked rocker which signals that Tull are back for the attack. The wittily titled 'Kissing Willie' (geddit?!) suggests they're adequately equipped to match Horse (London) in the penile jousting stakes, and it sees Tull's trademark staccato blunderbuss tempo refined to a new intensity. Watch out, Metallica!"

"After the opening salve, *Rock Island* adopts familiar forms. With this title and the preceding *Crest Of A Knave*, it's safe to say that Tull are dedicated to the preservation of the Great Prog Rock Pun. The "ethnic" tinges have once again been dropped for a *Knave*-style rock fundamentalism, while commercial aspects have skilfully been grafted on. Tull's stolid rockclunkiness is cheerfully oblivious to the over and undertones of today's most incandescent guitar music. But so what? This is exactly how the band and their fans want it. Tull's brand of frumpy eclecticism lives on, from the bluesy strains of 'The Rattlesnake Trail' to 'Ears Of Tin' and 'Another Christmas Song', which both boast a Knopfleresque vocal rasp and a vein of subdued sentimentality."

"Despite their age-old "folk" elements, Tull evoke the seventies far more than the ancient times they align themselves with. It's this that makes them such an endearingly quaint modern antique. Their trusty scheme continues with *Rock Island* — the fans'll love it while the rest of us smile indulgently and pass, on to a DIY sporran kit and a Dinosaur Jr. album."

From *Raw* magazine: "Jethro Tull — riding breeches, blinking monocles, wittering flutes, fish farms an' all — are the kind of band you either love or hate… The band's last effort, 87's *Crest Of A Knave*, was their best for years, adopting a rockier, more guitar orientated sound than its immediate synth-handed predecessors. All Tullites will be pleased to know that *Rock Island* jigs around in a similar vein. The vibe is a familiar one: a rural setting, the sun sinking, neckerchiefs loosely knotted, tweed jackets unbuttoned, and the strains of flutes and mandolins swirling around Ian Anderson's bug-eyed vocals and Martin Barre's carefully carved guitar work. Hardly Saturday night on Sunset Strip stuff, but a trusty formula that continues to yield worthy additions to the Tull roster."

"Openers 'Kissing Willie' and 'The Rattlesnake Trail' kick-start the thing with tails up and ears down. 'Ears Of Tin' plods methodically in their wake, while 'Undressed To Kill' adopts a gentler tone whilst recounting a tale of ashamed lust. Over on the flip, 'The Whaler's Dues' brings out the concerned environmentalist in writer/

engineer/producer Ian Anderson, while 'Heavy Water' shapes up as one of the album's finest moments. 'Another Christmas Song', however, sounds a little too much like Dire-Straits-meets-James-Galway for comfort. Still, I'll deliberate no further. Fans of the band will no doubt have grabbed themselves a slice of *Rock Island* already, whilst those still sulking about the Grammy decision will be fuming into their Perrier."

From *Q* magazine: "*Rock Island* continues in much the same musical vein as *Crest Of A Knave* — ten songs performed with the skill you'd expect from this bunch of senior statesmen. There's less acoustic guitar than before, and less solo grandstanding, so the feel is much more of an ensemble performance, though Martin Barre's electric guitar and Ian Anderson's hustle-bustle flute are well to the fore. More significantly, Anderson's voice seems to have lost some of the uncertainty and dodgy Knopfleresque intonation he adopted on the last album. Meanwhile, honest Dave Pegg plucks both bass and mandolin beautifully, underrated Doane Perry thumps the tubs, and the imposing Maartin Allcock doubles on guitars and keyboards."

"Favourite Tull themes emerge blinking into the sunlight again — the vigour of the country versus the decay of the city ('Ears Of Tin'), our limitless facility for fucking up ('Heavy Water' and 'The Whaler's Dues'), sex ('Undressed To Kill') and, of course, Christmas. Two of the out-and-out rockers deserve a mention here. 'Kissing Willie' is a wonderfully sleazy tale of oral sex in market towns ('Willie stands and Willie falls/Willie hangs his head behind grey factory walls,' whoops Anderson cheerfully), and 'The Rattlesnake Trail' fair scalds along thanks to Barre's needle-sharp riffing."

"'The Whaler's Dues' is probably the strongest song here. Over a repetitive guitar and flute hook, Anderson takes the part of said salty old dog bemoaning the demise of the whale — not because of any late conversion to conservation, but because in the end there was nothing left for him to kill. Other stand-outs are the title track (hats off to Peter Vettese guesting on keyboards) and 'Strange Avenues', and it's here, if you like, that the wheel comes full circle. Stepping into his warm limo, our hero observes: 'The wino sleeps, cold coat lined with the money section/Looking like a record cover from 1971'. Indeed. Tull tour the UK again from September 18th, and the crowds are going to eat this up."

***

For the tour to promote *Rock Island*, Jethro Tull incorporated a unique stage production element for 'Kissing Willie' that involved the use of projected silhouettes of lithe dancers. The performance culminated with a potentially controversial image that some may have considered to be bordering on pornographic.

In October 1989, under the heading of "Jethro Tull May Be A Dinosaur Band, But It Still Can Rock," *The Boston Globe* reviewed a performance that took place at The Worcester Centrum: "It's not easy being a Jethro Tull fan these days. You find yourself defending a band that is, let's face it, unfashionable — one that people still tend to see as arena-rock dinosaurs. That's been especially true in the past year since Tull, who aren't really a heavy metal group, snatched the hard rock/heavy metal Grammy from such hipper choices as Jane's Addiction and Metallica. Keep in mind, however, that Jethro Tull was always the nonconformist of arena bands, the one that tried plenty of odd ideas — album-length songs, fusions with English folk music, pop songs questioning the nature of God — and made them work. Still the only major rock band fronted by a flautist who likes to stand on one leg, Tull was still doing its usual tricks before a crowd of ten-thousand on Saturday — and doing them proud."

"Tull sounded especially sprightly this year, having ditched the show-off keyboard players from recent line-ups. After playing 'Steel Monkey', leader Ian Anderson made the night's only reference to the controversy: 'You remember that one, it's from our heavy metal album'. Parts of the show still sounded like Tull's response to the Grammy flap: You want heavy metal, we'll give you heavy metal. To these ears, the current *Rock Island* is one of the half-dozen best Tull albums, with more warmth and more kick than anything they've done in at least a decade. And they featured the album on Saturday, which meant that lead guitarist Martin Barre got to show what a powerhouse he can be. It also meant that Anderson got to sing some of his more resonant lyrics. 'The Whaler's Dues' was a rarity, an ecologically-minded song with some real venom to it. And pretty 'Another Christmas Song' set up a friendly mood that felt completely unforced."

"Also noticeable were some acoustic surprises, including the ballad 'Jack-A-Lynn' and a set of folk dance tunes with Doane Perry on Irish drum, and Dave Pegg and Maartin Allcock (who both double as members of the folk-rock band Fairport Convention) on mandolin and bouzouki. Though much of the set was newish material, they dug up some rarely played oldies, including the good-natured 'Nothing Is Easy' and the darker 'My God', with Anderson shaking a fist at the heavens. The one thing about Tull that can't be defended is the occasional bit of sexist humour. The single, 'Kissing Willie', is within bounds — it's funny and it rocks — but it didn't need to be illustrated with slides that looked like *Penthouse* rejects. Also regrettable was Anderson during 'Budapest', gawking at a scantily-clad woman who turned up on stage. Tull didn't play like a bunch of dirty old men, so they don't have to act like one."

Writing for *Sounds*, in October 1989, journalist Sam King reviewed a performance that took place at the Hammersmith Odeon: "The last time I was here, three-thousand pre-pubescent waifs ripped their lungs out to Bros' immature wheezing. Tonight, for Jethro Tull, the contrast couldn't have been greater. No screaming, no cavorting kids, and no hint of airborne knickers. But then the Tull could hardly be considered inspiring. Their seventeen-year-old *Thick As A Brick* extends the progressive flute solo to new heights, while "new" songs like 'The Whaler's Dues' merely force home their points with an aged inevitability that only bands like Tull, Yes and Floyd really possess."

"Old and gnarly, Tull are the equivalent of a crusty pair of thermal leggings — Ian Anderson even models a pair on stage. He's the centrepoint of Tull's musical immobility, their stoic timelessness and awesome stability. They're a musical leviathan, an unmoving blend of Tolkien folkiness, ghastly progressive rock and atrocious visual puns. A massive extension of schoolboy sexism and failed humour, most noticeable during 'Christmas

Song'. They're everything '76 was against, the inspiration behind All About Eve's wafty forest fairies. The saddest thing is that in an age of Stones and Who re-runs, Jethro Tull's dreary double-decade stodge — typified by their latest *Rock Island* LP — seems totally in keeping with the times. Retrogression has never seemed so unbearable. Across town, The New Fast Automatic Daffodils were playing their evil modern music. We missed out."

The following week, in response to Sam King's negative review and overall derogatory remarks about Jethro Tull, several fans who had written to *Sounds* in complaint of this had their letters printed in the publication. The fan response to King's review is not only demonstrative of the fact that there was a divide between Tull fans and the music press on this one occasion, but plausibly throughout the entirety of the eighties. It makes sense that many writing for the music press across the decade may have felt obliged to express a negative attitude towards Jethro Tull — in line with what they perhaps thought their editors and/or readers may have been expecting. Whilst it would be unrealistic to insist that all bad reviews of Jethro Tull's efforts were unfair or inaccurate, it is important to take into account what the fans were saying. For they, after all — whether long-time supporters since the late sixties, or of a younger generation who had begun liking the band at a later stage — were the ones who were buying the records and the concert tickets, giving the band a level of support that signified that it was far from game over for Jethro Tull.

"Whose bright idea was it to let Sam King loose on Jethro Tull's gig at the Hammersmith Odeon? His own, probably. Ho ho ho, Sam," wrote Darryl McSorley of

London. "So Tull are old, eh? Well, so are your parents, or have you stopped talking to them now they are not so old and "trendy" like you? No, I bet you haven't, because if you did, they would stop your pocket money. You say Tull are everything '76 was against. You pillock. How old were you in 1976? Twelve? Jethro Tull were making music a darn sight more revolutionary and provocative in 1976 than so-called "punks" like Siouxsie And The Banshees, Talking Heads, and Slaughter And The Dogs. Listen to *Songs From The Wood* if you don't believe me. Finally, twerp features, you say New Fast Automatic Daffodils were playing that night. Well, I've never fucking heard of them, I don't have any of their albums and think their name is stupid. But you don't see me doing a review on them, do you? No, because I'm not a trendy cretin like you. And anyway, Tull were playing that night and I had a ticket. I would have paid twenty times the asking price to see Tull because Tull are fucking ace. So up your jacksy, Sam King."

"Recently in Birmingham and London, like Sam King, I too saw Jethro Tull," wrote Anon. "And your review was perhaps an attempt to impress what I assume is your general audience — juveniles. I have never heard of Sam King. I know your paper even less. But I have heard of Jethro Tull. They are in demand in England (nine shows sold out), the USA, Germany, Italy, Brazil, and Australia. *Crest Of A Knave* sold one-point-three-million copies. *Rock Island* will sell likewise. Ian Anderson is a millionaire. Dave Pegg and Martin Barre both have recording studios and promote new groups. So, as Tull begin another US tour after twenty-one years, I expect they worry greatly about Sam King's next review."

Said Graham Maisey of Surrey; "Your reviewer, Sam King, may not like Jethro Tull, but apparently quite a few people do, as they have just completed a sellout tour of the UK — including three consecutive nights at the Hammersmith Odeon. I doubt very much if the Automatic Daffodils could do that, or even if they will be around to celebrate their twenty-first anniversary."

Some of the fairest reviews are perhaps the ones that reference what the audience got out of a performance. Such was the case when in November 1989, the *Tampa Bay Times* reviewed Jethro Tull's performance at the University of South Florida's Sun Dome; "In the footsteps of The Who and the tire tracks of the Rolling Stones, folk-rock fogey Jethro Tull became the final British rock retreads to reach Tampa this concert season. After twenty-one years, singer-flautist Ian Anderson is both the band's focal point and its only historical link to its beginnings. His moodiness reportedly resulted in a half-hearted performance in Orlando on Saturday night. On Sunday at the University of South Florida Sun Dome, Anderson and his bandmates gave a comfortable and familiar, if uninspired, performance."

"Jethro Tull quickly showed its ability to fill a hall with noise during the openers, 'Strange Avenues' and 'Steel Monkey'. That point proven, Anderson returned to the meandering Olde English folk rock that made his a most distinctive sound in the 1970s. A muddy sound system and Anderson's craggy voice rendered some lyrics unintelligible, but long-time fans filled in the gaps by singing along. Many could name tunes such as 'Thick As A Brick 'and 'Nothing Is Easy' after two acoustic guitar chords. Many songs kicked off with extended and pretentious overtures, but were ultimately faithful to the originals."

"The two-hour set was marked by wild swings from medieval folk to bass-laden bombast. Anderson led the way with his sorcerer's presence and sliding vocal phrasings. At forty-two, he isn't as lithe as in his younger days, unless you count his flute-playing. Snorting and singing into the microphoned instrument, Anderson showed that he is far from ready to roll over and die musically."

Although it was subject to change, the setlist for the *Rock Island* tour is demonstrative of how by the end of the eighties, Jethro Tull had plenty of new material to be proud of, but there was also an abundance of older songs that continued to be played with pride and affection. For instance, here's the setlist from 8th December 1989, which was performed for the band's show at the San Diego Sports Arena:

Strange Avenues
Steel Monkey
Thick As A Brick
Rock Island
Requiem
Black Satin Dancer
Cheap Day Return
Mother Goose
Jack-A-Lynn
Another Christmas Song
My God
The Pine Marten's Jig
Drowsy Maggie

The Whaler's Dues
Budapest
Farm On The Freeway
Sealion
Kissing Willie
Nothing Is Easy
Aqualung
Wind-Up
Locomotive Breath
The Third Hoorah

The fact that songs from the seventies and the eighties are still included in Jethro Tull setlists to this very day speaks volumes of how both decades have been of relevance — not just to the band, but to the fans as well.

***

Out of the eighties and into a new decade, *Catfish Rising* was released in 1991. Although it was labelled as being a "return to playing the blues," the album features abundant use of mandolin and acoustic guitar. Also, there is less use of keyboards than on any Jethro Tull album of the eighties. In that regard, *Catfish Rising* certainly signifies that following the eighties, the band were ready to leave behind some of the stylistic elements that had featured on their albums from that period.

"I've actually come to loathe and detest electronic and synthesised noises," Anderson explained as part of the *Catfish Rising* press release. "What interests me more at the moment is to get back to music that grows on trees — instruments that you actually have to play, as opposed to sitting down and reading some two-hundred-page manual in order to play a part. A lot of the songs on *Crest Of A Knave* and *Rock Island* were written on keyboards, but all of the songs on the new album were written on guitar or mandolin, and that gives them a completely different flavour."

For *Catfish Rising*, the Anderson-led line-up maintained Martin Barre, Dave Pegg and Doane Perry. Along with other additional musicians on keyboards, Andrew Giddings made his Tull debut on the album. Staying with the band until 2007, he is Jethro Tull's longest serving keyboard player to date.

Dave Pegg left Jethro Tull during the band's recording of the 1995 album, *Roots To Branches*. In doing so, he chose to focus on Fairport Convention.

Also a long-standing member of Jethro Tull, Doane Perry stayed with them up until 2011 prior to the band going on hiatus. Later that year, Martin Barre told journalists that there were no current plans for future Jethro Tull work. In 2012, he assembled and toured with a new group. Billed as Martin Barre's New Day, the band played mostly Jethro Tull material. Barre continues to enjoy a solo career.

Following several albums, releases, tours, and new line-ups under the Jethro Tull name, the Ian Anderson-fronted Jethro Tull is still going strong to this day, with their new album, *RökFlöte*, having been released in April 2023.

As an absolute minimum, for fans who aren't too keen on the 1980s Jethro Tull output, the fact is, that it kept the band's name going across a range of explorations into new musical styles and themes. Overall though, there is arguably so much more to Jethro Tull's eighties music in terms of how it still features so many of the wonderful characteristics that made the band's music so endearing in the seventies, and in the late sixties before that.

When it comes to deciding upon which Jethro Tull album to listen to at any given moment, it is understandable that some might prefer to reach for what they consider to be the more "classic" version of the band — whether that be *Benefit*, *Thick As A Brick* or *Songs From The Wood*. But does the idea of "classic" Jethro Tull include some — or all — of their albums from the eighties? Well, perhaps not for everyone. But for those who want to give the technological explorations that feature on *A* and *Under Wraps* a chance, or for those who want to hear the fantasy-themed lyrics and folk-inspired melodies on *The Broadsword And The Beast*, or for anyone who wants to hear the heavy rock on *Crest Of A Knave* and *Rock Island*, there is certainly a tremendous offering of fascinating music to be enjoyed.

Discography

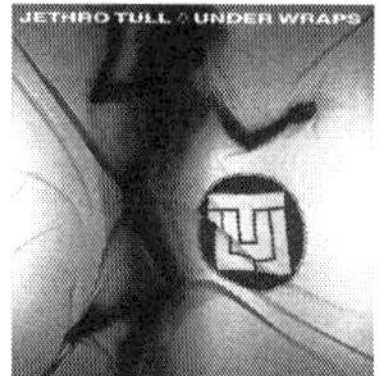

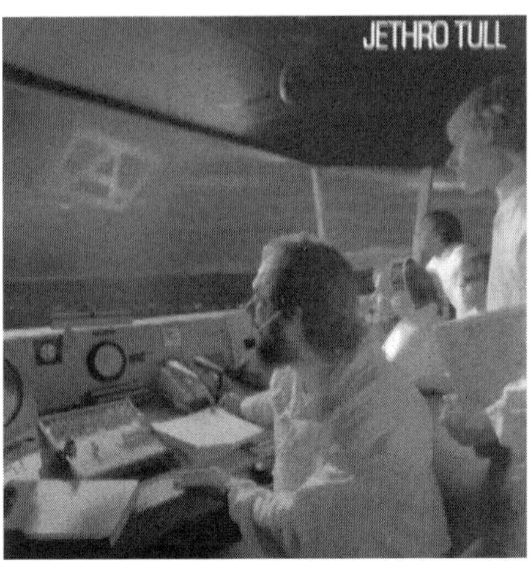

A

(1980)

All tracks written by Ian Anderson with additional music material from Eddie Jobson.
Arranged by Jethro Tull.

Side One
1. Crossfire (3:55)
2. Fylingdale Flyer (4:35)
3. Working John, Working Joe (5:04)
4. Black Sunday (6:35)

Side Two
1. Protect And Survive (3:36)
2. Batteries Not Included (3:52)
3. Uniform (3:34)
4. 4.W.D. (Low Ratio) (3:42)
5. The Pine Marten's Jig (instrumental) (3:28)
6. And Further On (4:21)

Personnel

Ian Anderson – vocals, flute
Martin Barre – guitar
Dave Pegg – bass guitar, mandolin
Mark Craney – drums

Eddie Jobson – keyboards, synthesiser, electric violin on 'The Pine Marten's Jig'

Robin Black – sound engineer
John Shaw – photography
Peter Wagg – art direction

The Broadsword And The Beast
(1982)

All tracks are written by Ian Anderson with additional material by Peter-John Vettese.

Side One – Beastie
1. Beastie (3:58)
2. Clasp (4:18)
3. Fallen On Hard Times (3:13)
4. Flying Colours (4:39)
5. Slow Marching Band (3:40)

Side Two – Broadsword
1. Broadsword (5:03)
2. Pussy Willow (3:55)
3. Watching Me, Watching You (3:41)
4. Seal Driver (5:10)
5. Cheerio (1:09)

Personnel

Ian Anderson – lead vocals, flute, acoustic guitar,
Fairlight CMI
Martin Barre – acoustic guitar, electric guitar
Dave Pegg – backing vocals, bass guitar, mandolin
Peter-John Vettese – backing vocals, keyboards,
piano, synthesiser
Gerry Conway – drums, percussion

Robin Black – sound engineering
Jim Gibson – artwork
Leigh Mantle – assistant engineer
Iain McCaig – artwork, illustrations
Paul Samwell-Smith – producer

Walk Into Light
(1983)
(Ian Anderson's solo album)

Side One
1. Fly By Night (Ian Anderson, Peter-John Vettese (3:55)
2. Made In England (Anderson, Vettese) (5:00)
3. Walk Into Light (Anderson) (3:11)
4. Trains (Anderson, Vettese) (3:21)
5. End Game (Anderson) (3:20)

Side Two
1. Black And White Television (Anderson) (3:37)
2. Toad In The Hole (Anderson) (3:24)
3. Looking For Eden (Anderson) (3:43)
4. User-Friendly (Anderson, Vettese) (4:03)
5. Different Germany (Anderson, Vettese) (5:24)

Personnel

Ian Anderson – producer, engineer, vocals, flute, guitar, bass, keyboards, artwork, design concept
Peter-John Vettese – keyboards

John Pasche – art direction
Martyn Goddard – photography

The Cocktail Cowboy Goes It Alone
(1983)
(Dave Pegg's solo album)

Side One
1. The Cocktail Cowboy (Dave Pegg) (3:05)
2. Jack Frost And The Hooded Crow (Ian Anderson) (3:15)
3. Barnes Morris (Ralph McTell) (2:29)
4. All The Dance Numbers (Glen Gardier) (4:00)
5. The Swirling Pit (Pegg) (3:28)
6. Pipe Major Jock Laidlaws Fancy (Pegg) (2:58)

Side Two
1. The Journeymen (Steve Ashley) (4:06)
2. Carolans Draught (arrangement by Dave Pegg) (3:50)
3. Level Pegging (Traditional, arr. Pegg) (3:03)
4. Song For Sandy (Pegg) (4:04)
5. Lord Mayo (Trad., arr. Pegg) (4:54)

Personnel

Dave Pegg – all instruments and vocals, producer, engineer, sleeve notes

Mark Powell – engineer
Simon Graty – engineer
Boppin' Bob – lacquer cutting
Mick O'Toole – cover
John Woodward – photography

Dave takes a lighthearted look at home

Dave Pegg has long been loved by Birmingham fans for his work with Fairport Convention and Jethro Tull. He still plays with both groups — but now he's going it alone as well, as the title of his new solo album will tell you.

Called *The Cocktail Cowboy Goes It Alone*, it's a folk/rock/comedy offering which gently pokes fun at his native Brum.

There are also songs on it by Jethro Tull's lead singer Ian Anderson, and folk Ralph McTell.

Dave recorded the album at the small studio in his home in Banbury, and took the cover pictures in a Banbury pub.

And now he is planning to play some of the numbers with a six-piece group, who have their debut date at The Motorhouse Hotel in Banbury on July 29.

Dave said: "I've been wanting to do this for ages, but I've never really had time.

"Since Jethro Tull appeared at the NEC a year ago we've done a 42-date tour of America, which was pretty gruelling, and we've also been to Germany where we headlined with Neil Young.

"After that we had to stop for a while, and Ian started working

by JACKIE BAILEY

on a solo project, so I was able to get down to this.

"I love the folk circuit in Britain, because everybody knows everyone else and it's very friendly. It's a nice break from playing huge concert halls."

Dave has a chance soon to link up with the old friends again, as he's busy helping to organise the annual Fairport Convention reunion concert.

The concert will be part of a two-day festival at Home Farm in Cropredy on August 12 and 13, with top folk artists from all over the country.

But in September it's back to heavier rock again, when he starts rehearsing with Jethro Tull for a 1984 album and tour.

Dave Pegg, pictured during his days with chart-topping Birmingham band Fairport Convention.

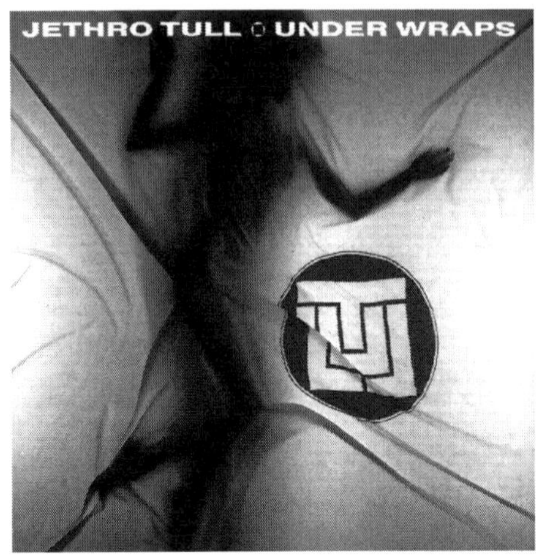

Under Wraps
(1984)

All tracks are written by Ian Anderson and Peter-John Vettese except where indicated.

Side One
1. Lap Of Luxury (Anderson) (3:35)
2. Under Wraps #1 (Anderson) (3:59)
3. European Legacy (Anderson) (3:23)
4. Later, That Same Evening (3:51)
5. Saboteur (3:31)
6. Radio Free Moscow (3:40)

Side Two
1. Nobody's Car (Anderson, Martin Barre, Vettese) (4:08)
2. Heat (5:37)
3. Under Wraps #2 (Anderson) (2:14)
4. Paparazzi (Anderson, Barre, Vettese) (3:47)
5. Apogee (5:28)

CD

1. Lap Of Luxury (Anderson) (3:35)
2. Under Wraps #1 (Anderson) (3:59)
3. European Legacy (Anderson) (3:23)
4. Later, That Same Evening (3:51)
5. Saboteur (3:31)
6. Radio Free Moscow (3:40)
7. Astronomy (3:38)
8. Tundra (3:41)
9. Nobody's Car (Anderson, Barre, Vettese) (4:08)
10. Heat (5:37)
11. Under Wraps #2 (Anderson) (2:14)
12. Paparazzi (Anderson, Barre, Vettese) (3:47)
13. Apogee (5:28)
14. Automotive Engineering (4:05)
15. General Crossing (4:02)

Personnel

Ian Anderson – vocals, flute, acoustic guitar,
drum programming, Fairlight CMI
Martin Barre – electric guitar
Dave Pegg – bass guitar, double bass
Peter-John Vettese – keyboards, electronic programming

Trevor Key – cover photo, photography
John Pasche – artwork, cover design
Sheila Rock – photography

A Classic Case
(1985)

Side One
1. Locomotive Breath (4:16)
2. Thick As A Brick (4:24)
3. Elegy (3:41)
4. Bourée (3:10)
5. Fly By Night (4:12)

Side Two
1. Aqualung (6:22)
2. Too Old To Rock 'n' Roll: Too Young To Die (3:27)
3. Teacher/Bungle In The Jungle/Rainbow Blues/Locomotive Breath (3:58)
4. Living In The Past (3:29)
5. War Child (4:56)

Personnel

Ian Anderson – flute, acoustic guitar
Martin Barre – electric guitar
Dave Pegg – bass guitar
Peter-John Vettese – keyboards
Paul Burgess - drums, percussion
London Symphony Orchestra
Dee Palmer – orchestral arrangements

Crest Of A Knave
(1987)

All tracks written by Ian Anderson.

Side One
1. Steel Monkey (3:39)
2. Farm On The Freeway (6:31)
3. Jump Start (4:55)
4. She Said She Was A Dancer (3:43)

Side Two
1. Budapest (10:05)
2. Mountain Men (6:20)
3. Raising Steam (4:05)

CD

1. Steel Monkey (3:39)
2. Farm On The Freeway (6:31)
3. Jump Start (4:55)
4. She Said She Was A Dancer (3:43)
5. Dogs In The Midwinter (4:37)
6. Budapest (10:05)
7. Mountain Men (6:20)
8. The Waking Edge (4:49)
9. Raising Steam (4:05)

Personnel

Ian Anderson – vocals, flute, acoustic guitar, electric guitar, additional percussion, keyboards, Synclavier, drum programming (on tracks 1, 5 and 9)
Martin Barre – acoustic guitar, electric guitar
Dave Pegg – bass guitar, acoustic bass (on track 4)

Doane Perry – drums, percussion (on tracks 2 and 7)
Gerry Conway – drums, percussion (on tracks 3, 4, 6 and 8)
Ric Sanders – violin (on tracks 6 and 8)

Robin Black – engineer
Andrew Jamieson – artwork, calligraphy
Tim Matyear – engineer
John Pasche – art direction
Stephen W. Tayler – engineer, remixing

Rock Island
(1989)

All tracks written by Ian Anderson.

Side One
1. Kissing Willie (3:32)
2. The Rattlesnake Trail (4:02)
3. Ears Of Tin (4:55)
4. Undressed To Kill (5:25)
5. Rock Island (6:54)

Side Two
1. Heavy Water (4:12)
2. Another Christmas Song (3:32)
3. The Whaler's Dues (7:53)
4. Big Riff And Mando (5:58)
5. Strange Avenues (4:10)

Personnel

Ian Anderson – vocals, flute, acoustic guitar, keyboards, Synclavier, mandolin, drums, percussion (on 'The Rattlesnake Trail' and 'Another Christmas Song')
Martin Barre – acoustic guitar, electric guitar
Dave Pegg – bass guitar, acoustic bass, mandolin
Doane Perry – drums, percussion

Maartin Allcock – keyboards (on 'Kissing Willie' and 'Strange Avenues')
Peter-John Vettese – additional keyboards (on 'Ears Of Tin' through to 'Heavy Water')
Jim Gibson – illustrations
Mark Tucker – mixing

Tour Dates

Please be aware that the following list may not be exhaustive. Conflicting accounts exist of Jethro Tull's tour dates. Consequently, the list here is derived from corroboration of information from posters, ticket stubs and reviews.

From August 1979 to June 1980, the members of Jethro Tull were Ian Anderson, Martin Barre, John Evan, Barriemore Barlow, David Palmer and Dave Pegg.

1980

13th March	The Drammenhallen Mars, Drammen, Norway
14th March	Istadion, Stockholm, Sweden
16th March	Congresgebouw, Hague, Holland
17th March	Voorst National, Brussels, Belgium
18th March	Saarlandhalle, Saarbrucken, Germany
19th March	Frederich Ebert Halle, Ludwigshafen, Germany
20th March	Munsterlandhalle, Munster, Germany
22nd March	Deutschlandhalle, Berlin, Germany
23rd March	Congress Centrum Halle 1, Hamburg, Germany
24th March	Kuppelsaal, Hannover, Germany
25th March	Eissporthalle, Kassel, Germany
26th March	Sporthalle, Cologne, Germany
28th March	Stadthalle, Bremen, Germany
29th March	Philipshalle, Dusseldorf, Germany
30th March	Grugahalle, Essen, Germany
31st March	Böblingen Sporthalle, Böblingen, Germany
1st April	Olympiahalle, Munich, Germany
2nd April	Festhalle, Frankfurt, Germany

3rd April	Hallenstadion, Zurich, Switzerland
4th April	Palais Des Sporte, Dijon, France
8th April	Apollo, Glasgow, Scotland
9th April	ABC Apollo, Manchester, England
10th April	Hammersmith Odeon, London, England
11th April	Hammersmith Odeon, London, England
12th April	Hammersmith Odeon, London, England
13th April	Hammersmith Odeon, London, England
14th April	Hammersmith Odeon, London, England

From June 1980 to May 1981, the members of Jethro Tull were Ian Anderson, Martin Barre, Dave Pegg, Mark Craney and Eddie Jobson.

4th October	State College, Salisbury MD., USA
5th October	Capital Centre, Landover MD., USA
6th October	Civic Centre, Hartford CT., USA
7th October	Utica Memorial Auditorium, Utica NY., USA
8th October	Madison Square Garden, New York, USA
9th October	Madison Square Garden, New York, USA
10th October	Civic Centre, Providence RI., USA
11th October	Boston Tea Gardens, Boston MA., USA
12th October	Nassau Coliseum, Uniondale NY., USA
13th October	Spectrum, Philadelphia PA., USA
15th October	Richfield Coliseum, Cleveland OH., USA
16th October	Riverfront Coliseum, Cincinnati OH., USA
17th October	Saginaw Civic Centre, Saginaw MI., USA
18th October	Milwaukee Arena, Milwaukee WI., USA
19th October	Rosemont Horizon, Chicago IL., USA
20th October	Civic Centre, St Paul MN., USA
22nd October	Detroit Cobo Hall, Detroit MI., USA
23rd October	Wings Stadium, Kalamazoo MI., USA
24th October	Uni Of Illinois Assembly Hall, Champaign IL., USA
25th October	Gardens, Louisville KY., USA
26th October	Checkerdome, St Louis MO., USA
28th October	Municipal Auditorium, Kansas City MO., USA

29th October	Tulsa Assembly Centre, Tulsa OK., USA
30th October	Lloyd Noble Arena, Norman OK., USA
31st October	Reunion Arena, Dallas TX., USA
1st November	Convention Centre Arena, San Antonio TX., USA
2nd November	Sam Houston Coliseum, Houston TX., USA
3rd November	Sam Houston Coliseum, Houston TX., USA
4th November	Tingley Coliseum, Albuquerque NM., USA
5th November	McNichols Arena, Denver CO., USA
7th November	Swing Auditorium, San Bernardino CA., USA
8th November	Selland Arena, Fresno CA., USA
9th November	Oakland Coliseum, Oakland CA., USA
10th November	San Diego Sports Arena, San Diego CA., USA
11th November	Sports Arena, Los Angeles CA., USA
12th November	Sports Arena, Los Angeles CA., USA
20th November	Royal Albert Hall, London, England
21st November	Royal Albert Hall, London, England

1981

1st February	Voorst National, Brussels, Belgium
2nd February	Sporthalle, Böblingen, Germany
3rd February	Festhalle, Frankfurt, Germany
4th February	Ahoy, Rotterdam, Holland
5th February	Westfalenhalle, Dortmund, Germany
7th February	Scandinavium, Gonburg, Sweden
8th February	Forum, Copenhagen, Denmark
9th February	Congress Centrum Halle, Hamburg, Germany
10th February	Congress Centrum Halle, Hamburg, Germany
11th February	Messesportpalast, Hannover, Germany
12th February	Stadthalle, Bremerhaven, Germany
13th February	Munsterlandhalle, Munster, Germany
14th February	Sporthalle, Cologne, Germany
16th February	Deutschlandhalle, Berlin, Germany
17th February	Freiheithalle, Hof, Germany
18th February	Sporthalle, Augsburg, Germany
19th February	Nibelungenhalle, Passau, Germany
20th February	Rudi Sedlmeyerhalle, Munich, Germany
21st February	Fredrich Eberthalle, Ludwigshafen, Germany
22nd February	Saarlandhalle, Saarbrucken, Germany
23rd February	Hippodrome, Paris, France
24th February	Des Sportes, Lyon, France

From June 1981 to December 1983, the members of Jethro Tull were Ian Anderson, Martin Barre, Dave Pegg, Peter Vettese and Gerry Conway or Paul Burgess.

1982

1st April	Drammenshallen, Drammen, Norway
2nd April	Isstadion, Stockholm, Sweden
3rd April	Tivoli Konsertsal, Copenhagen, Denmark
4th April	Stadthalle, Bremen, Germany
5th April	Deutschlandhale, Berlin, Germany
6th April	Olympiahalle, Munich, Germany
7th April	Fredrich-Ebert-Halle, Ludwigshafen, Germany
8th April	Congress Centrum Halle, Hamburg, Germany
9th April	Kuppelsaal, Hannover, Germany *Cancelled*
10th April	Congress Centrum Halle, Hamburg, Germany *Cancelled*
11th April	Sporthalle, Cologne, Germany
12th April	Grugahalle, Essen, Germany
13th April	Saarlandhalle, Saarbrucken, Germany
14th April	Palais Des Sports, Lyons, France
15th April	Maison Des Sport, Cermont-Ferrand, France
16th April	Palais Des Sports, Dijon, France
17th April	Theatre De Verdure, Nice, France
19th April	??, Montpellier, France
21st April	??, Nantes, France
22nd April	Hippodrome De Pantin, Paris, France
25th April	Voorst National, Brussels, Belgium
26th April	Festhalle, Frankfurt, Germany
27th April	Nibelungenhalle, Passau, Germany
29th April	Sporthalle, Böblingen, Germany
30th April	Stadthalle, Freiburg, Germany
2nd May	7-Up Theatre, Rome, Italy
3rd May	Palasport, Bologna, Italy
4th May	Palasport, Genova, Italy
5th May	Palazzo Dello Sport, Padova, Italy
6th May	Theatrede Verdur, Nice, France
7th May	Municipal De Deportes, Barcelona, Spain
8th May	Real Madrid Indoor Hall, Madrid, Spain
9th May	Velodromo De Auneta, San Sebastian, Spain

11th May	Ahoy, Rotterdam, Holland
13th May	Wembley Arena, London, England
14th May	Playhouse, Edinburgh, Scotland
15th May	City Hall, Newcastle, England
16th May	National Exhibition Centre, Birmingham, England
17th May	Cornwall Coliseum, St Austell, England
19th May	Inverness Ice Rink, Inverness, Scotland
28th May	Westfallenhalle, Dortmund, Germany
21st July	Dominion Theatre (The Prince's Trust Gala), London, England
28th August	Nostel Priory (Theakston Festival), Wakefield, England
1st September	Plaza De Toros, Barcelona, Spain
4th September	Reinwiessen Festival, Wiesbaden, Germany
5th September	Nuremburg Festival, Nuremburg, Germany
9th September	Merriwear Post Pavilion, Columbia MD., USA
10th September	War Memorial Hall, Rochester NY., USA
11th September	Blossom Music Centre, Cuyahoga Falls OH., USA
12th September	Poplar Creek Music Centre, Hoffman Estates IL., USA
14th September	Pine Knob Music Centre, Clarkson MI., USA
15th September	Pine Knob Music Centre, Clarkson MI., USA
16th September	Hara Arena, Dayton OH., USA
17th September	Civic Arena, Pittsburgh PA., USA
18th September	Nassau Coliseum, Uniondale NY., USA
19th September	Civic Centre, Glens Falls NY., USA
21st September	Spectrum, Philadelphia PA., USA
22nd September	War Memorial Auditorium, Buffalo NY., USA
23rd September	Maple Leaf Gardens, Toronto, Canada
24th September	Montreal Forum, Montreal, Canada
26th September	City Coliseum, Quebec City, Canada
28th September	Veterans Memorial Coliseum, New Haven CT., USA
29th September	Civic Centre, Portland ME., USA
30th September	Meadowlands Arena, East Rutherford NJ., USA
1st October	Broome County Arena, Binghampton NY., USA
2nd October	Worcester Centrum, Worcester ME., USA
3rd October	Civic Centre, Providence RI., USA
5th October	Hampton Rhodes Coliseum, Hampton Rhodes VA., USA

6th October	Charlotte Coliseum, Charlotte NC., USA
7th October	Omni, Atlanta GA., USA
8th October	O'Connell Centre, University Of Florida, Gainsville FL., USA
9th October	Hollywood Sportatorium, Miami FL., USA
10th October	Bayfront Centre, St Petersburg FL., USA
12th October	Leon County Arena, Tallahassee FL., USA
13th October	Lakefront Arena, New Orleans LA., USA
14th October	Summit, Houston TX., USA
15th October	San Antonio Centre Arena, San Antonio TX., USA
16th October	Reunion Arena, Dallas TX., USA
17th October	Folsom Field, Boulder CO., USA
19th October	Oakland Coliseum Arena, Oakland CA., USA
20th October	LA Memorial Sports Arena, Inglewood CA., USA
21st October	Swing Auditorium, San Bernardino CA., USA
22nd October	Selland Arena, Fresno CA., USA
23rd October	Lawlor Event Centre, Reno NV., USA
24th October	Fox Theatre, Stockton CA., USA

From 1984 to 1987, the members of Jethro Tull were Ian Anderson, Martin Barre, Dave Pegg, Peter Vettese and Doane Perry.

1984

30th August	Caird Hall, Dundee, Scotland
1st September	Apollo, Glasgow, Scotland
2nd September	City Hall, Newcastle, England
3rd September	Apollo, Manchester, England
4th September	Apollo, Manchester, England
6th September	National Exhibition Centre, Birmingham, England
7th September	Hammersmith Odeon, London, England
8th September	Hammersmith Odeon, London, England
9th September	Hammersmith Odeon, London, England
12th September	Palacio Municipal Deportes, Barcelona, Spain
13th September	Crudad Portiva Del Real Madrid, Madrid, Spain
14th September	Velodromo Anoeta, San Sebastian, Spain
15th September	Palais Des Sportes, Toulouse, France
16th September	Les Arenas, Orange, France
17th September	Le Zenith, Paris, France
18th September	Salle Omnisport, Renes, France
21st September	Konserthuset, Stockholm, Sweden
22nd September	Falkoner Theatret, Copenhagen, Denmark
24th September	Congresgebouw, The Hague, Holland
25th September	Voorst National, Brussels, Belgium
26th September	Sporthalle, Cologne, Germany
27th September	Rhein Neckar Halle, Heidelberg, Germany
28th September	Schleyerhalle, Stuttgart, Germany
29th September	Festhalle, Frankfurt, Germany
30th September	Grugahalle, Essen, Germany
2nd October	Congress Centrum Halle, Hamburg, Germany
3rd October	Congress Centrum Halle, Hamburg, Germany
4th October	International Congress Centrum, Berlin, Germany
6th October	Olympiahalle, Munich, Germany
7th October	Hallenstadion, Zurich, Germany
12th October	Veterans Memorial Coliseum, New Haven CT., USA
13th October	Meadowlands Arena, East Rutherford NJ., USA
14th October	Broome County Arena, Binghampton NY., USA

16th October	Richfield Coliseum, Cleveland OH., USA
17th October	War Memorial Coliseum, Rochester NY., USA
18th October	Civic Centre, Baltimore MD., USA
19th October	Spectrum, Philadelphia PA., USA
20th October	Buffalo War Memorial Auditorium, Buffalo NY., USA
21st October	Ottawa Civic Centre, Ottawa, Canada
22nd October	Forum, Montreal, Canada
23rd October	Maple Leaf Gardens, Toronto, Canada
24th October	Coliseum, Quebec, Canada
26th October	Nassau Coliseum, Uniondale NY., USA
27th October	Civic Centre, Providence RI., USA
28th October	Capital Theatre, Passaic NJ., USA
29th October	Centrum, Worcester MA., USA
31st October	Pittsburgh Civic Centre, Pittsburgh PA., USA
1st November	Veterans Auditorium, Columbus OH., USA
2nd November	Dane County Coliseum, Madison WI., USA
3rd November	Joe Louis Arena, Detroit MI., USA
4th November	Chicago UIC Pavilion, Chicago IL., USA
5th November	St Paul Civic Centre, St Paul MN., USA
8th November	Lakefront Arena, New Orleans LA., USA
9th November	Convention Centre, San Antonio TX., USA
10th November	Sam Houston Coliseum, Houston TX., USA
11th November	Reunion Arena, Dallas TX., USA *Cancelled*
13th November	Boulder Events Centre, Boulder CO., USA
14th November	Salt Palace Arena, Salt Lake City UT.,USA
17th November	PNE Coliseum, Vancouver BC., Canada
18th November	Arena, Seattle WA., USA
19th November	Coliseum, Portland OR., USA
21st November	Cow Palace, San Francisco CA., USA
22nd November	Universal Amphitheatre, Los Angeles CA.,USA
23rd November	Universal Amphitheatre, Los Angeles CA., USA *Cancelled*
5th December	Sports And Entertainment Centre, Melbourne, Australia
10th December	Entertainment Centre, Sydney, Australia
11th December	Entertainment Centre, Sydney, Australia
13th December	Festival Hall, Brisbane, Australia

16th December	Entertainment Centre, Sydney, Australia
18th December	Sports And Entertainment Centre, Melbourne, Australia

1985

16th March	International Congress Centrum, Berlin, Germany J.S. Bach Tri-Centenary Concert with Eddie Jobson.

1986

28th June	Bowl, Milton Keynes, England
30th June	Hayarkon Park, Tel Aviv, Israel
2nd July	Mkt Stadium (Old Gymnasium), Budapest, Hungary
4th July	Midtfyns Festival, Ringe, Denmark
5th July	Out In The Green Festival, Inselwiese, Dinkelsbühl, Germany
6th July	Lorelei Freilichtbuhne, St Goarhausen, Germany

1987

15th August	Cropredy Festival, England Ian Anderson and Martin Barre guest appearance.

From September 1987 to December 1987, the members of Jethro Tull were Ian Anderson, Martin Barre, Dave Pegg, Don Airey and Gerry Conway or Doane Perry.

4th October	Playhouse, Edinburgh, Scotland
5th October	City Hall, Newcastle, England
7th October	ABC Apollo, Manchester, England
8th October	ABC Apollo, Manchester, England
9th October	National Exhibition Centre, Birmingham, England

JETHRO TULL
LONDON DATE – SOLD OUT
NEC TICKETS AVAILABLE
BIRMINGHAM NEC
Friday 9th October at 8pm
Tickets £8.50 £7.50 available from the NEC Box Office, credit card bookings 021 780 4133 and Keith Prowse Credit Card Hotline 01-741 8989 (subject to booking fee).

11th October	Congresgebouw, The Hague, Holland
12th October	Cirque Royale, Brussels, Belgium
14th October	Carl Diem Halle, Würzburg, Germany
15th October	Schleyer Halle, Stuttgart, Germany
16th October	Hallenstadion, Zurich, Switzerland
18th October	Sporthalle, Hamburg, Germany
19th October	Rhein Neckar Halle, Heidelberg, Germany
20th October	Olympiahalle, Munich, Germany
22nd October	ICC, Berlin, Germany
23rd October	Sporthalle, Cologne, Germany
24th October	Grugahalle, Essen, Germany
26th October	Le Zenith, Paris, France
27th October	Festhalle, Frankfurt, Germany
29th October	Hammersmith Odeon, London, England
7th November	Civic Centre, Providence RI., USA
10th November	Troy Fieldhouse, Troy NY., USA
11th November	Civic Centre, Baltimore MD., USA
13th November	Nassau Coliseum, Uniondale NY., USA
14th November	Coliseum, New Haven CT., USA
15th November	Mid Hudson Civic Centre, Poughkeepsie NY., USA
16th November	Stabler Arena, Allentown PA., USA
17th November	Civic Centre, Providence RI., USA
19th November	Maple Leaf Gardens, Toronto, Canada
20th November	Forum, Montreal, Canada
21st November	1:00pm set for Hungerthon in New York NY., USA
21st November	Centrum, Worcester MA., USA
22nd November	Meadowlands Arena, East Rutherford NJ., USA
24th November	Tower Theatre, Philadelphia PA., USA
25th November	Tower Theatre, Philadelphia PA., USA
27th November	Cobo Arena, Detroit MI., USA
28th November	Cleveland Public Hall, Cleveland OH., USA
29th November	Pavilion, Chicago IL., USA
1st December	Forum, St Paul MN., USA
2nd December	Arena, Milwaukee WI., USA
3rd December	Fox Theatre, St Louis MO., USA
5th December	McNichols Arena, Denver CO., USA

7th December   Salt Palace Arena, Salt Lake City UT., USA
9th December   Arena, Seattle WA. USA
10th December   Schnitzer Auditorium, Portland OR., USA
12th December   Arco Arena, Sacramento CA., USA
13th December   Civic Auditorium, San Francisco CA., USA
14th December   Universal Amphitheatre, Los Angeles CA., USA
15th December   Universal Amphitheatre, Los Angeles CA.,USA
16th December   Universal Amphitheatre, Los Angeles CA., USA
17th December   Golden Hall, San Diego, USA *Cancelled*

From January 1988 to December 1991, the members of Jethro Tull were Ian Anderson, Martin Barre, Dave Pegg, Maartin Allcock and Doane Perry.

1988

1st June	Shoreline Amphitheatre, Mountain View CA., USA
2nd June	Pavilion, Concord CA., USA
3rd June	Irvine Meadows Amphitheatre, Laguna Hills CA., USA
5th June	State University Open Air Theatre, San Diego CA., USA
7th June	Red Rocks Amphitheatre, Denver CO., USA
9th June	Convention Centre Arena, Dallas TX., USA
10th June	Zoo Amphitheatre, New Orleans LA., USA
12th June	Poplar Creek Music Theatre, Hoffman Estates IL., USA
13th June	Blossom Music Centre, Cuyahoga Falls OH., USA
14th June	Pine Knob Music Theatre, Clarkson MI., USA
16th June	Chastian Memorial Park Amphitheatre, Atlanta GA., USA
17th June	Mud Island, Memphis TN., USA
19th June	Kings Dominion Showplace, Roswell VA.,USA
20th June	Riverbend Music Centre, Cincinnati OH., USA
21st June	Merriweather Post Pavilion, Columbia MD., USA
23rd June USA.	Great Woods Performing Arts Centre, Mansfield MA., USA.
24th June	Jones Beach Theatre, Wantagh NY., USA
25th June	Performing Arts Amphitheatre, Saratoga Springs NY., USA
26th June	FR Mann Music Centre, Philadelphia PA., USA
27th June	Pier 84, New York NY., USA
3rd July	Plazzo Del Civilta Del Lavoro, Rome, Italy
4th July	Plazza De Santa Croce, Florence, Italy
5th July	Palstrussardi, Milan, Italy
6th July	Comunal Arena, Corregio, Italy
8th July	Tent On Village Green, Imst, Austria
9th July	Volkspark Dutzendteich, Nuremberg, Germany
10th July	Open Air Festival, Frauenfeld, Switzerland
12th July	Open Air Arena, Vienna, Austria
13th July	Mkt Stadium, Budapest, Hungary

15th July	??, Athens, Greece
16th July	Vfb Stadion (Waldstadion), Giessen, Germany
17th July	Open Air, Walsrode, Germany *Cancelled*
19th July	Wembley Arena, London, England
26th July	Belo Horizonte, Belo, Brazil
2nd August	Gigantinho, Porto Allegre, Brazil
6th August	Maracananzinho, Sao Paulo, Brazil
7th August	Maracananzinho, Sao Paulo, Brazil
8th August	Maracananzinho, Sao Paulo, Brazil
30th August	Maracananzinho, Rio De Janeiro, Brazil

1989

16th August	Cropredy Festival, England
	Ian Anderson and Martin Barre guest appearance.
18th September	Eden Court Theatre, Inverness, Scotland
20th September	City Hall, Newcastle, England
21st September	Playhouse, Edinburgh, Scotland
23rd September	ABC Apollo, Manchester, England
24th September	ABC Apollo, Manchester, England
25th September	National Exhibition Centre, Birmingham, England
27th September	Hammersmith Odeon, London, England
28th September	Hammersmith Odeon, London, England
29th September	Hammersmith Odeon, London, England
1st October	Hamburg Sporthalle, Hamburg, Germany
2nd October	Eilenriedenhalle, Hannover, Germany
3rd October	Festhalle, Frankfurt, Germany
5th October	Liederhalle, Stuttgart, Germany
6th October	Olympiahalle, Munich, Germany
7th October	Karl Dien Halle, Würzburg, Germany
9th October	Grugahalle, Essen, Germany
10th October	Sporthalle, Cologne, Germany
11th October	Frederich Eberthalle, Ludwigshafen, Germany
13th October	Hallenstadion, Zurich, Switzerland
14th October	Halle Des Fetes, Lausanne, Switzerland
15th October	Palatrussardi, Milan, Italy
16th October	Palasport, Turin, Italy
23rd October	RPI Fieldhouse, Troy NY., USA
24th October	War Memorial, Rochester NY., USA
26th October	Hamilton Copps Arena, Hamilton, Canada
27th October	Forum, Montreal, Canada.
28th October	Centrum, Worcester MA., USA
29th October	Cumberland Civic Centre, Portland ME., USA
31st October	New Haven Coliseum, New Haven CT., USA
1st November	Civic Centre, Providence RI., USA

2nd November	Spectrum, Philadelphia PA., USA
3rd November	Nassau Coliseum, Uniondale NY., USA
4th November	Coliseum, Richmond VA., USA
6th November	Palace, Auburn Hills MA., USA
7th November	Public Hall, Cleveland OH., USA
8th November	Palumbo Centre, Pittsburgh PA., USA
9th November	Meadowlands Arena, East Rutherford NJ., USA
11th November	Hill Auditorium, Ann Arbor MI., USA
12th November	Veterans Auditorium, Columbus OH., USA
14th November	Arie Crown Theatre, Chicago IL., USA
15th November	Chicago Theatre, Chicago IL., USA
16th November	Redbird Arena, Normal IL., USA
17th November	Forum, St Paul MN., USA
19th November	Riverfront Coliseum, Cincinnati OH., USA
20th November	Fox Theatre, St Louis MO., USA
21st November	Von Braun Civic Centre, Huntsville AL., USA
22nd November	Omni, Atlanta GA., USA
23rd November	Convention Centre, Orlando FL., USA
24th November	James L Knight Centre, Miami FL., USA
26th November	Sun Dome, Tampa FL., USA
28th November	Lakefront Arena, New Orleans LA., USA
29th November	Summit, Houston TX., USA
30th November	State Fair Coliseum, Dallas TX., USA
1st December	City Civic Centre, Oklahoma City OK., USA
3rd December	McNichols Arena, Denver CO., USA
5th December	Universal Amphitheatre, Los Angeles CA.,USA
6th December	Universal Amphitheatre, Los Angeles CA.,USA
7th December	Compton Terrace, Phoenix AZ., USA
8th December	San Diego Sports Arena, San Diego CA.,USA
10th December	San Francisco Civic Auditorium, San Francisco CA.,USA